William Alexander Clouston

The Book of Noodles

Stories of Simpletons, or, Fools and Their Follies

William Alexander Clouston

The Book of Noodles
Stories of Simpletons, or, Fools and Their Follies

ISBN/EAN: 9783744751438

Printed in Europe, USA, Canada, Australia, Japan

Cover: Foto ©Lupo / pixelio.de

More available books at **www.hansebooks.com**

STORIES OF SIMPLETONS;
FOOLS AND THEIR FOLLIE

BY

W. A. CLOUSTO

Author of "Popular Tales and Fictions: their
Transformations."

"Excellent! Why, this is the best fooling when all
is done."—*Twelfth Night.*

LONDON ·
ELLIOT STOCK, 62, PATERNOSTER ROW.

PREFACE.

*L*IKE *popular tales in general, the original sources of stories of simpletons are for the most part not traceable. The old Greek jests of this class had doubtless been floating about among different peoples long before they were reduced to writing. The only tales and apologues of noodles or stupid folk to which an approximate date can be assigned are those found in the early Buddhist books, especially in the " Játakas," or Birth-stories, which are said to have been related to his disciples by Gautama, the illustrious founder of Buddhism, as incidents which occurred to himself and others in former births, and were afterwards put into a literary form by his followers. Many* *of the "Játakas" relate to silly men and women, and also to stupid animals, the latter being, of course, men re-born as beasts, birds, or reptiles. But it is not to be supposed that all are of Buddhist invention; some had doubtless been current for ages among the Hindús before Gautama promulgated his mild doctrines. Scholars are, however, agreed that these fictions date at latest from a century prior to the Christian era.*

Of European noodle-stories, as of other folk-tales, it may be said that, while they are numerous, yet the elements of which they are composed are comparatively very few. The versions domiciled in different countries exhibit little originality, farther than occasional modifications in accordance with local manners and customs. Thus for the stupid Bráhman of Indian stories the blundering, silly son is often substituted in European variants; for the brose in Norse and Highland tales we find polenta or macaroni in Italian and Sicilian versions. The identity of incidents in the noodle-stories of Europe with those in what are for us their oldest forms, the Buddhist and Indian books, is very remarkable, particularly so in the case of Norse popular fictions, which, there is every reason to believe, were largely introduced through the Mongolians ; and the similarity of Italian and West Highland stories to those of Iceland and Norway would seem to indicate the influence of the Norsemen in the Western Islands of Scotland and in the south of Europe.

It were utterly futile to attempt to trace the literary history of most of the noodle-stories which appear to have been current throughout European countries for many generations, since they have practically none. Soon after the invention of printing collections of facetiæ were rapidly multiplied, the compilers taking their material from oral as well as written sources, amongst others, from mediæval collections of " exempla " designed for the use of preachers and the writings of the classical authors of antiquity. With the exception of those in Buddhist works, it is more than probable that the noodle-stories which are found among all peoples never had any other purpose than that of mere amusement. Who, indeed, could possibly convert the "witless devices" of the men of Gotham into vehicles of moral instruction? Only the monkish writers of the Middle Ages, who even "spiritualised" tales which, if reproduced in these days, must be "printed for private circulation"!

Yet may the typical noodle of popular tales "point a moral," after a fashion. Poor fellow! he follows his instructions only too literally, and with a firm conviction that he is thus doing a very clever thing. But the consequence is almost always ridiculous. He practically shows the fallacy of the old saw that "fools learn by experience," for his next folly is sure to be greater than the last, in spite of every caution to the contrary. He is generally very honest, and does

everything, like the man in the play,
"with the best intentions." His mind is
incapable of entertaining more than one
idea at a time; but to that he holds fast,
with the tenacity of the lobster's claw:
he cannot be diverted from it until, by
some accident, a fresh idea displaces it;
and so on he goes from one blunder to
another. His blunders, however, which
in the case of an ordinary man would
infallibly result in disaster to himself or
to others, sometimes lead him to unexpected good fortune. He it is, in fact,
to whom the great Persian poet Sádi
alludes when he says, in his charming
"Gulistán," or Rose Garden, "The al-
chemist died of grief and distress, while
the blockhead found a treasure under
a ruin." Men of intelligence toil pain-
fully to acquire a mere "livelihood";
the noodle stumbles upon great wealth
in the midst of his wildest vagaries.
In brief, he is—in stories, at least—a
standing illustration of the "vanity of
human life." 1

*And now a few words as to the history
and design of the following work. When
the Folk-lore Society was formed, some
nine years since, the late Mr. W. J.
Thoms, who was one of the leading men
in its formation, promised to edit for the
Society the "Merry Tales of the Mad Men
of Gotham," furnishing notes of analogous
stories, a task which he was peculiarly
qualified to perform. As time passed on,
however, the infirmities of old age doubtless rendered the purposed work less and
less attractive to him, and his death, after
a long, useful, and honourable career, left
it still undone. What particular plan he
had sketched out for himself I do not
know ; but there can be no doubt that
had he carried it out the results would
have been most valuable. And, since he
did not perform his self-allotted task, his
death is surely a great loss, perhaps an
irreparable loss, to English students of
comparative folk-lore.*

*More than five years ago, with a view
of urging Mr. Thoms to set about the*

work, I offered to furnish him with some material in the shape of Oriental noodle-stories; but from a remark in his reply I feared there would be no need for such services as I could render him. That fear has been since realised, and the present little book is now offered as a humble substitute for the intended work of Mr. Thoms, until it is displaced by a more worthy one.

Since the " Tales of the Men of Gotham " ceased to be reproduced in chap-book form, the first reprint of the collection was made in 1840, with an introduction by Mr. J. O. Halliwell (now Halliwell-Phillipps); and that brochure is become almost as scarce as the chap-book copies themselves : the only copy I have seen is in the Euing collection in the Glasgow University Library. The tales were next reprinted in the " Shakespeare Jest-books," so ably edited and annotated by Mr. W. Carew Hazlitt, in three volumes (1864). They were again reproduced in Mr. John

Ashton's " Chap-books of the Eighteenth
Century " (1882).

It did not enter into the plan of any
of these editors to cite analogues or
variants of the Gothamite Tales ; nor,
on the other hand, was it any part of
my design in the present little work to
reproduce the Tales in the same order
as they appear in the printed collection.
Yet all that are worth reproducing in a
work of this description will be found in
the chapters entitled " Gothamite Drolleries," of which they form, indeed, but
a small portion.

My design has been to bring together,
from widely scattered sources, many of
which are probably unknown or inaccess-
ible to ordinary readers, the best of this
class of humorous narratives, in their
oldest existing Buddhist and Greek forms
as well as in the forms in which they are
current among the people in the present
day. It will, perhaps, be thought by
some that a portion of what is here
presented might have been omitted with-

*out great loss ; but my aim has been not
only to compile an amusing story-book,
but to illustrate to some extent the
migrations of popular fictions from country to country. In this design I was
assisted by Captain R. C. Temple, one
of the editors of the " Indian Antiquary,"
and one of the authors of " Wide-awake
Stories," from the Panjáb and Kashmir,
who kindly directed me to sources whence I
have drawn some curious Oriental paral-
lels to European stories of simpletons.*

W. A. C.

*** *While my " Popular Tales and Fictions "
was passing through the press, in* 1886, *I made
reference (in vol. i., p.* 65) *to the present work, as
it was purposed to be published that year, but Mr.
Stock has had unavoidably to defer its publication
till now.*

W. A. C.

GLASGOW, *March,* 1888.

CONTENTS

CHAPTER I.

ANCIENT GRECIAN NOODLES . . . 1-15

PAGE

CHAPTER II.

GOTHAMITE DROLLERIES :

Reputed communities of stupids in different
countries—The noodles of Norfolk: their
lord's bond; the dog and the honey;
the fool and his sack of meal—Tales of
the Mad Men of Gotham : Andrew Borde
not the author—The two Gothamites at
Notts Bridge—The hedging of the cuckoo
—How the men of Gotham paid their
rents — The twelve fishers and the
courtier—The *Gúrú Paramartan*—The
brothers of Bakki—Drowning the eel—
The Gothamite and his cheese—The
trivet—The buzzard—The gossips at

PAGE

the alehouse—The cheese on the highway—The wasp's nest—Casting sheep's
eyes—The devil in the meadow—The
priest of Gotham—The "boiling" river
— The moon a green cheese — The
"carles of Austwick"—The Wiltshire
farmer and his pigs .   .   .   16-55

CHAPTER III.

GOTHAMITE DROLLERIES *(continued)* :

The men of Schilda : the dark council-house ;
the mill-stone; the cat — Sinhalese
noodles: the man who observed Buddha's five precepts—The fool and the
Rámáyana—The two Arabian noodles—
The alewife and her hens—"Sorry he
has gone to heaven"—The man of Hama
and the man of Hums—*Bizarrures* of
the Sieur Gaulard—The rustic and the
dog   56-80

CHAPTER IV.

GOTHAMITE DROLLERIES *(continued)* ·

The simpleton and the sharpers—The schoolmaster's lady-love—The judge and the
thieves—The calf's head—The Kashmírí
and his store of rice—The Turkish

PAGE

noodle : the kerchief ; the caftan ; the
wolf's tail ; the right hand and the left ;
the stolen cheese ; the moon in the well
—The good dreams—Chinese noodles :
the lady and her husband ; the stolen
spade ; the relic-hunter—Indian noodles :
the fools and the mosquitoes ; the fools
and the palm-trees ; the servants and
the trunks ; taking care of the door ; the
fool and the aloes-wood ; the fool and
the cotton ; the cup lost in the sea ; the
fool and the thieves ; the simpletons who
ate the buffalo ; the princess who was
made to grow ; the washerman's ass
transformed ; the foolish herdsman—
Noodle-stories moralised—The brothers
and their heritage — Sowing roasted
sesame   .   .   .   81-120

CHAPTER V.

The Silly Son :

Simple Simon—The Norse booby — The
Russian booby—The Japanese noodle—
The Arabian idiot—The English silly
son—The Sinhalese noodle with the
robbers—The Italian booby—The Arab
simpleton and his cow—The Russian
fool and the birch-tree—The silly wife

PAGE

deceived by her husband—The Indian
fool on the tree-branch—The Indian
monk who believed he was dead—The
Florentine fool and the young men—
The Indian silly son as a fisher; as a
messenger; killing a mosquito; as a
pupil—The best of the family—The
doctor's apprentice . . . 121-170

CHAPTER VI.

THE FOUR SIMPLE BRÁHMANS :

Introduction 171
Story of the first Bráhman 176
Story of the second Bráhman . . 178
Story of the third Bráhman . . . 181
Story of the fourth Bráhman . . 185
Conclusion 190

CHAPTER VII.

THE THREE GREAT NOODLIS . . 191-218

APPENDIX.

JACK OF DOVER'S QUEST OF THE FOOL OF
ALL FOOLS 219

THE BOOK OF NOODLES.

CHAPTER I

ANCIENT GRECIAN NOODLES.

"OLD as the days of Hierokles!" is the exclamation of the "classical" reader on hearing a well-worn jest; while, on the like occasion, that of the "general" reader—a comprehensive term, which, doubtless, signifies one who knows "small Latin and less Greek"—is, that it is "a Joe Miller;" both implying that the critic is too deeply versed in *joke-ology* to be imposed upon, to have an old jest palmed on him as new, or as one made by a living wit. That the so-called jests of Hierokles are *old* there can be no doubt whatever; that they were collected by the Alexandrian sage of that name is more than doubtful; while it is certain that several of them are much older than the time in which he flourished, namely, the fifth century: it is very possible that some

I

may date even as far back as the days of
the ancient Egyptians! It is perhaps hardly
necessary to say that honest Joseph Miller,
the comedian, was not the compiler of the
celebrated jest-book with which his name
is associated; that it was, in fact, simply a
bookseller's trick to entitle a heterogeneous
collection of jokes, "quips, and cranks, and
quiddities," *Joe Miller's Jests; or, The Wits
Vade Mecum.* And when one speaks of a
jest as being "a Joe Miller," he should only
mean that it is "familiar as household words,"
not that it is of contemptible antiquity,
albeit many of the jokes in "Joe Miller" are,
at least, "as old as Hierokles," such, for
instance, as that of the man who trained his
horse to live on a straw *per diem*, when it
suddenly died, or that of him who had a
house to sell and carried about a brick as
a specimen of it.

The collection of facetiæ ascribed to
Hierokles, by whomsoever it was made, is
composed of very short anecdotes of the sayings and doings of pedants, who are represented as noodles, or simpletons. In their
existing form they may not perhaps be of
much earlier date than the ninth century.
They seem to have come into the popular
facetiæ of Europe through the churchmen of
the Middle Ages, and, after having circulated

long orally, passed into literature, whence, like other kinds of tales, they once more returned to the people. We find in them the indirect originals of some of the bulls and blunders which have in modern times been credited to Irishmen and Scotch Highlanders, and the germs also, perhaps, of some stories of the Gothamite type : as brave men lived before Agamemnon, so, too, the race of Gothamites can boast of a very ancient pedigree ! By far the greater number of them, however, seem now pithless and pointless, whatever they may have been considered in ancient days, when, perhaps, folk found food for mirth in things which utterly fail to tickle our "sense of humour" in these double-distilled days. Of the 'Aστεῖα, or facetiæ, of Hierokles, twenty-eight only are appended to his Commentary on Pythagoras and the fragments of his other works edited, with Latin translations, by Needham, and published at Cambridge in 1709. A much larger collection, together with other Greek jests—of the people of Abdera, Sidonia, Cumæ, etc.—has been edited by Eberhard, under the title of *Philogelos Hieraclis et Philagrii Facetiæ*, which was published at Berlin in 1869.

In attempting to classify the best of these relics of ancient wit—or witlessness, rather—it is often difficult to decide whether a particular jest is of the Hibernian bull, or blunder, genus or an example of that droll stupidity which is the characteristic of noodles or simpletons. In the latter class, however, one need not hesitate to place the story of the men of Cumæ, who were expecting shortly to be visited by a very eminent man, and having but one bath in the town, they filled it afresh, and placed an open grating in the middle, in order that half the water should be kept clean for his sole use.

But we at once recognise our conventional Irishman in the pedant who, on going abroad, was asked by a friend to buy him two slave-boys of fifteen years each, and replied, " If I cannot find such a pair, I will bring you one of thirty years ; " and in the fellow who was quarrelling with his father, and said to him, " Don't you know how much injury you have done me ? Why, had you not been born, I should have inherited my grandfather's estate;" also in the pedant who heard that a raven lived two hundred years, and bought one that he should ascertain the fact for himself.

Among Grecian Gothamites, again, was the hunter who was constantly disturbed by dreams of a boar pursuing him, and procured dogs to sleep with him. Another, surely, was the man of Cumæ who wished to sell some clothes he had stolen, and smeared them with pitch, so that they should not be recognised by the owner. They were Gothamites, too, those men of Abdera who punished a runaway ass for having got into the gymnasium and upset the olive oil. Having brought all the asses of the town together, as a caution, they flogged the delinquent ass before his fellows.

Some of the jests of Hierokles may be considered either as witticisms or witless sayings of noodles; for example, the story of the man who recovered his health though the doctor had sworn he could not live, and afterwards, being asked by his friends why he seemed to avoid the doctor whenever they were both likely to meet, he replied, "He told me I should not live, and now I am ashamed to be alive;" or that of the pedant who said to the doctor, "Pardon me for not having been sick so long;" or this, "I dreamt that I saw and spoke to you last night:" quoth the other, "By the gods, I was so busy, I did not hear you."

But our friend the Gothamite reappears in the pedant who saw some sparrows on a tree, and went quietly under it, stretched out his robe, and shook the tree, expecting to catch the sparrows as they fell, like ripe fruit; again, in the pedant who lay down to sleep, and, finding he had no pillow, bade his servant place a jar under his head, after stuffing it

full of feathers to render it soft ; again, in
the cross-grained fellow who had some honey
for sale, and a man coming up to him and
inquiring the price, he upset the jar, and then
replied, " You may sh:d my heart's blood like
that before I tell such as you ; " and again,
in the man of Abdera who tried to hang himself, when the rope broke, and he hurt his
head ; but after having the wound dressed by
the doctor, he went and accomplished his
purpose. And we seem to have a trace of
them in the story of the pedant who dreamt
that a nail had pierced his foot, and in the
morning he bound it up ; when he told a
friend of his mishap, he said, " Why do you
sleep barefooted ? "

The following jest is spread—*mutatis
mutandis*—over all Europe: A pedant, a bald
man, and a barber, making a journey in company, agreed to watch in turn during the
night. It was the barber's watch first. He
propped up the sleeping pedant, and shaved
his head, and when his time came, awoke him.
When the pedant felt his head bare, " What
a fool is this barber," he cried, " for he has
roused the bald man instead of me ! "

A variant of this story is related of a raw
Highlander, fresh from the heather, who put
up at an inn in Perth, and shared his bed
with a negro. Some coffee-room jokers hav-

ing blackened his face during the night, when
he was called, as he had desired, very early
next morning, and got up, he saw the reflection
of his face in the mirror, and exclaimed in
a rage, "Tuts, tuts! The silly body has
waukened the wrang man."

In connection with these two stories may
be cited the following, from a Persian jest-
book: A poor wrestler, who had passed all
his life in forests, resolved to try his fortune
in a great city, and as he drew near it he
observed with wonder the crowds on the road,
and thought, "I shall certainly not be able to
know myself among so many people if I have
not something about me that the others have
not." So he tied a pumpkin to his right leg,
and, thus decorated, entered the town. A
young wag, perceiving the simpleton, made
friends with him, and induced him to spend
the night at his house. While he was asleep,
the joker removed the pumpkin from his leg
and tied it to his own, and then lay down
again. In the morning, when the poor fellow
awoke and found the pumpkin on his companion's leg, he called to him, "Hey! get up,
for I am perplexed in my mind. Who am I,
and who are you? If I am myself, why is
the pumpkin on your leg? And if you are
yourself, why is the pumpkin not on my leg?"

Modern counterparts of the following jest

are not far to seek: Quoth a man to a pedant,
"The slave I bought of you has died." Rejoined the other, "By the gods, I do assure
you that he never once played me such a
trick while I had him." The old Greek
pedant is transformed into an Irishman, in
our collections of facetiæ, who applied to a
farmer for work. "I'll have nothing to do
with you," said the farmer, "for the last five
Irishmen I had all died on my hands." Quoth
Pat, "Sure, sir, I can bring you characters
from half a dozen gentlemen I've worked for
that I never did such a thing." And the jest
is thus told in an old translation of *Les Contes
Facetieux de Sieur Gaulard*: "Speaking of
one of his Horses which broake his Neck at
the descent of a Rock, he said, Truly it was
one of the handsomest and best Curtalls in
all the Country; he neuer shewed me such
a trick before in all his life."[1]

Equally familiar is the jest of the pedant who
was looking out for a place to prepare a tomb

[1] Etienne Tabourot, the author of this amusing
little book, who was born at Dijon in 1549 and
died in 1590, is said to have written the tales in
ridicule of the inhabitants of Franche Comte, who
were then the subjects of Spain, and reputed to
be stupid and illiterate. From a manuscript
translation, entitled *Bigarrures; or, The Pleasant
and Witlesse and Simple Speeches of the Lord
Gaulard of Burgundy*, purporting to be made by

for himself, and on a friend indicating what he thought to be a suitable spot, "Very true," said the pedant, "but it is unhealthy." And we have the prototype of a modern "Irish" story in the following: A pedant sealed a jar of wine, and his slaves perforated it below and drew off some of the liquor. He was astonished to find his wine disappear while the seal remained intact. A friend, to whom he had communicated the affair, advised him to look and ascertain if the liquor had not been drawn off from below. "Why, you fool," said he, "it is not the lower, but the upper, portion that is going off."

It was a Greek pedant who stood before a mirror and shut his eyes that he might know how he looked when asleep—a jest which reappears in Taylor's *Wit and Mirth* in this form: "A wealthy monsieur in France (hauing profound reuenues and a shallow braine) was told by his man that he did continually gape

"J. B., of Charterhouse," probably about the year 1660, in the possession of Mr. Frederick William Cosens, London, fifty copies, edited, with a preface, by "A. S." (Alexander Smith), were printed at Glasgow in 1884. I am indebted to the courtesy of my friend Mr. F. T. Barrett, Librarian of the Mitchell Library, Glasgow, for directing my attention to this curious work, a copy of which is among the treasures of that already important institution.

in his sleepe, at which he was angry with his man, saying he would not belieue it.   His man verified it to be true; his master said that he would neuer belieue any that told him so, except (quoth hee) I chance to see it with mine owne eyes; and therefore I will have a great Looking glasse at my bed's feet for the purpose to try whether thou art a lying knaue or not." [1]

Not unlike some of our " Joe Millers" is the following: A citizen of Cumæ, on an ass, passed by an orchard, and seeing a branch of a fig-tree loaded with delicious fruit, he laid hold of it, but the ass went on, leaving him

---

[1] "*Wit and Mirth.*   Chargeably collected out of Taverns, Ordinaries, Innes, Bowling-greenes and Allyes, Alehouses, Tobacco-shops, Highwayes, and Water-passages.   Made up and fashioned into Clinches, Bulls, Quirkes, Yerkes, Quips, and Jerkes.   Apothegmatically bundled vp and garbled at the request of John Garrett's Ghost." (1635)—such is the elaborate title of the collection of jests made by John Taylor, the Water Poet, which owes very little to preceding English jest-books.   The above story had, however, been told previously in the *Bigarrures* of the Sieur Gaulard: "His cousine Dantressesa reproued him one day that she had found him sleeping in an ill posture with his mouth open, to order which for the tyme to come he commanded his seruant to hang a looking glasse upon the curtaine at his Bed's feet, that he might henceforth see if he had a good posture in his sleep."

suspended. Just then the gardener came up, and asked him what he did there. The man replied, "I fell off the ass."—An analogue to this drollery is found in an Indian story-book, entitled *Kathá Manjari:* One day a thief climbed up a cocoa-nut tree in a garden to steal the fruit. The gardener heard the noise, and while he was running from his house, giving the alarm, the thief hastily descended from the tree. "Why were you up that tree?" asked the gardener. The thief replied, "My brother, I went up to gather grass for my calf." "Ha! ha! is there grass, then, on a cocoa-nut tree?" said the gardener. "No," quoth the thief; "but I did not know; therefore I came down again."—And we have a variant of this in the Turkish jest of the fellow who went into a garden and pulled up carrots, turnips, and other kinds of vegetables, some of which he put into a sack, and some into his bosom. The gardener, coming suddenly on the spot, laid hold of him, and said, "What are you seeking here?" The simpleton replied, "For some days past a great wind has been blowing, and that wind blew me hither." "But who pulled up these vegetables?" "As the wind blew very violently, it cast me here and there; and whatever I laid hold of in the hope of saving myself remained in my hands." "Ah," said the gardener,

" but who filled this sack with them ? " " Well, that is the very question I was about to ask myself when you came up."

The propensity with which Irishmen are credited of making ludicrous bulls is said to have its origin, not from any lack of intelligence, but rather in the fancy of that lively race, which often does not wait for expression until the ideas have taken proper verbal form. Be this as it may, a considerable portion of the bulls popularly ascribed to Irishmen are certainly " old as the jests of Hierokles," and are, moreover, current throughout Europe. Thus in Hierokles we read that one of twin-brothers having recently died, a pedant, meeting the survivor, asked him whether it was he or his brother who had deceased.—Taylor has this in his *Wit and Mirth*, and he probably heard it from some one who had read the facetious tales of the Sieur Gaulard : "A noble-man of France (as he was riding) met with a yeoman of the Country, to whom he said, My friend, I should know thee. I doe remember I haue often seene thee. My good Lord, said the countriman, I am one of your Honers poore tenants, and my name is T. J. I remember better now (said my Lord); there were two brothers of you, but one is dead; I pray, which of you doth remaine aliue ? "—Mr. W. Carew Hazlitt, in the notes to his edition

of Taylor's collection (*Shakespeare Jest Books,*
Third Series), cites a Scotch parallel from
The Laird of Logan : "As the Paisley steamer
came alongside the quay[1] at the city of the
Seestus,[2] a denizen of St. Mirren's hailed one
of the passengers : 'Jock! Jock! distu
hear, man? Is that you or your brother?'"
And to the same point is the old nursery
rhyme,—

> "Ho, Master Teague, what is your story?
> I went to the wood, and killed a tory;[3]
> I went to the wood, and killed another :
> Was it the same, or was it his brother?"[4]

We meet with a very old acquaintance in
the pedant who lost a book and sought for it
many days in vain, till one day he chanced to
be eating lettuces, when, turning a corner, he
saw it on the ground. Afterwards meeting a
friend who was lamenting the loss of his
girdle, he said to him, "Don't grieve; buy
some lettuces; eat them at a corner; turn

[1] Only a Liliputian steamer could go up the
"river" Cart!
[2] "Seestu" is a nickname for Paisley, the good
folks of that busy town being in the habit of
frequently interjecting, "Seestu?"—*i.e.,* "Seest
thou?"—in their familiar colloquies.
[3] "Tory" is said to be the Erse term for a
robber.
[4] Halliwell's *Nursery Rhymes of England,*
vol. iv. of Percy Society's publications.

round it, go a little way on, and you will find
your girdle." But is there anything like this in
" Joe Miller " ?—Two lazy fellows were sleeping together, when a thief came, and drawing
down the coverlet made off with it. One of
them was aware of the theft, and said to the
other, " Get up, and run after the man that
has stolen our coverlet." " You blockhead,"
replied his companion, " wait till he comes
back to steal the bolster, and we two will
master him." And has " Joe " got this one ?—
A pedant's little boy having died, many friends
came to the funeral, on seeing whom he said,
" I am ashamed to bring out so small a boy
to so great a crowd."

An epigram in the *Anthologia* may find a
place among noodle stories :

" A blockhead, bit by fleas, put out the light,
  And, chuckling, cried, 'Now you can't see to
    bite!'"

This ancient jest has been somewhat im-
proved in later times. Two Irishmen in the
East Indies, being sorely pestered with mosquitoes, kept their light burning in hopes of
scaring them off, but finding this did not
answer, one suggested they should extinguish
the light and thus puzzle their tormentors to
find them, which was done. Presently the
other, observing the light of a firefly in the

room, called to his bedfellow, " Arrah, Mike, sure your plan's no good, for, bedad, here's one of them looking for us wid a lantern ! "

Our specimens may be now concluded with what is probably the best of the old Greek jokes. The father of a man of Cumæ having died at Alexandria, the son dutifully took the body to the embalmers. When he returned at the appointed time to fetch it away, there happened to be a number of bodies in the same place, so he was asked if his father had any peculiarity by which his body might be recognised, and the wittol replied, " He had a cough."

CHAPTER II.

T seems to have been common to most countries, from very ancient times, for the inhabitants of a particular district, town, or village to be popularly regarded as pre-eminently foolish, arrant noodles or simpletons. The Greeks had their stories of the silly sayings and doings of the people of Bæotia, Sidonia, Abdera, etc. Among the Perso-Arabs the folk of Hums (ancient Emessa) are reputed to be exceedingly stupid. The Kabaïl, or wandering tribes of Northern Africa, consider the Beni Jennad as little better than idiots. The Schildburgers are the noodles of German popular tales. In Switzerland the townsmen of Belmont, near Lausanne, are typical blockheads. And England has her "men of Gotham"—a village in Nottinghamshire—who are credited with most of the noodle stories which have been current among the people

for centuries past, though other places share to some extent in their not very enviable reputation: in Yorkshire the "carles" of Austwick, in Craven; some villages near Marlborough Downs, in Wiltshire; and in the counties of Sutherland and Ross, the people of Assynt.

But long before the men of Gotham were held up to ridicule as fools, a similar class of stories had been told of the men of Norfolk, as we learn from a curious Latin poem, *Descriptio Norfolciensium*, written, probably, near the end of the twelfth century, by a monk of Peterborough, which is printed in Wright's *Early Mysteries and Other Latin Poems.* This poem sets out with stating that Cæsar having despatched messengers throughout the provinces to discover which were bad and which were good, on their return they reported Norfolk as the most sterile, and the people the vilest and different from all other peoples. Among the stories related of the stupidity of the men of Norfolk is the following: Being oppressed by their lord, they gave him a large sum of money on condition that he should relieve them from future burdens, and he gave them his bond to that effect, sealed with a seal of green wax. To celebrate this, they all went to the tavern and got drunk. When it became dark, they

2

had no candle, and were puzzled how to procure one, till a clever fellow among the revellers suggested that they should use the wax seal of the bond for a candle—they should still have the words of the bond, which their lord could not repudiate; so they made the wax seal into a candle, and burned it while they continued their merry-making. This exploit coming to the knowledge of their lord, he reimposes the old burdens on the rustics, who complain of his injustice, at the same time producing the bond. The lord calls a clerk to examine the document, who pronounces it to be null and void in the absence of the lord's seal, and so their oppression continues.

Another story is of a man of Norfolk who put some honey in a jar, and in his absence his dog came and ate it all up. When he returned home and was told of this, he took the dog and forced him to disgorge the honey, put it back into the jar, and took it to market. A customer having examined the honey, declared it to be putrid. "Well," said the simpleton, "it was in a vessel that was not very clean."—Wright has pointed out that this reappears in an English jest-book of the seventeenth century. "A cleanly woman of Cambridgeshire made a good store of butter, and whilst she went a little way out

of the town about some earnest occasions,
a neighbour's dog came in in the meantime,
and eat up half the butter. Being come
home, her maid told her what the dog had
done, and that she had locked him up in the
dairy-house. So she took the dog and hang'd
him up by the heels till she had squeez'd all
the butter out of his throat again, whilst she,
pretty, cleanly soul, took and put it to the
rest of the butter, and made it up for Cambridge market. But her maid told her she
was ashamed to see such a nasty trick done.
' Hold your peace, you fool 1' says she ; ' 'tis
good enough for schollards. Away with it to
market 1 ' " '—Perhaps the original form is
found in the *Philogelos Hieraclis et Philagrii
Facetiæ*, edited by Eberhard. A citizen of
Cumæ was selling honey. Some one came up
and tasted it, and said that it was all bad.
He replied, "If a mouse had not fallen into
it, I would not sell it."

The well-known Gothamite jest of the
man who put a sack of meal on his own
shoulders to save his horse, and then got
on the animal's back and rode home, had
been previously told of a man of Norfolk,
thus :

¹ *Coffee House Jests.* Fifth edition. London.
1688. P. 36.

> "Ad foram ambulant diebus singulis;
> Saccum de lolio portant in humeris,
> Jumentis ne noccant: bene fatuis,
> Ut prolocutiis sum acquantur bestiis."

It reappears in the *Bigarrures* of the Sieur Gaulard:[1] "Seeing one day his mule charged with a verie great Portmantle, [he] said to his groome that was vpon the back of the mule, thou lasie fellowe, hast thou no pitie vpon that poore Beast? Take that port-mantle vpon thine owne shoulders to ease the poore Beast." And in our own time it is told of an Irish exciseman with a keg of smuggled whisky.

How such stories came to be transferred to the men of Gotham, it were fruitless to inquire.[2] Similar jests have been long current in other countries of Europe and throughout Asia, and accident or malice may have fixed the stigma of stupidity on any particular spot. There is probably no ground whatever for crediting the tale of the origin of the proverb, "As wise as the men

---

[1] See *ante*, p. 8, note.

[2] Fuller, while admitting that "an hundred fopperies are forged and fathered on the towns-folk of Gotham," maintains that "Gotham doth breed as wise people as any which laugh at their simplicity."

of Gotham," although it is reproduced in Thoroton's *Nottinghamshire*, i. 42-3:

" King John, intending to pass through this place, towards Nottingham, was prevented by the inhabitants, they apprehending that the ground over which a king passed was for ever after to become a public road. The King, incensed at their proceedings, sent from his court soon afterwards some of his servants to inquire of them the reason of their incivility and ill-treatment, that he might punish them. The villagers, hearing of the approach of the King's servants, thought of an expedient to turn away his Majesty's displeasure from them. When the messengers arrived at Gotham, they found some of the inhabitants engaged in endeavouring to drown an eel in a pool of water; some were employed in dragging carts upon a large barn to shade the wood from the sun; and others were engaged in hedging a cuckoo, which had perched itself upon an old bush. In short, they were all employed in some foolish way or other, which convinced the King's servants that it was a village of fools."

The fooleries ascribed to the men of Gotham were probably first collected and printed in the sixteenth century; but that jests of the "fools of Gotham" were current among the people long before that period is

evident from a reference to them in the *Wid-
kirk Miracle Plays*, the only existing MS.
of which was written about the reign of
Henry VI. :

> " Foles al sam ;
> Sagh I never none so fare
> Bote the foles of Gotham "

The oldest known copy of the *Merie Tales
of the Mad Men of Gotam* was printed
in 1630, and is preserved in the Bodleian
Library, Oxford. Warton, in his *History of
English Poetry*, mentions an edition, which
he says was printed about 1568, by Henry
Wikes, but he had never seen it. But Mr.
Halliwell (now Halliwell-Phillipps) in his
Notices of Popular English Histories, cites
one still earlier, which he thinks was probably
printed between 1556 and 1566: "Merie
Tales of the Mad Men of Gotam, gathered
together by A. B., of Phisike Doctour. [colo-
phon:] Imprinted at London, in Flet-Stret,
beneath the Conduit, at the signe of S. John
Evangelist, by Thomas Colwell, n. d. 12°,
black letter." The book is mentioned in *A
Briefe and Necessary Introduction*, etc., by
E. D. (8vo, 1572), among a number of other
folk-books : " Bevis of Hampton, Guy of
Warwicke, Arthur of the Round Table,
Huon of Bourdeaux, Oliver of the Castle,

The Four Sonnes of Amond, The Witles
Devices of Gargantua, Howleglas, Esop,
Robyn Hoode, Adam Bell, Frier Rushe, The
Fooles of Gotham, and a thousand such
other."[1] And Anthony à Wood, in his
Athenæ Oxonienses (1691-2), says it was
"printed at London in the time of K.
Hen. 8, in whose reign and after it was
accounted a book full of wit and mirth by
scholars and gentlemen. Afterwards being
often printed, [it] is now sold only on the
stalls of ballad-singers." It is likely that the
estimation in which the book was held "by
scholars and gentlemen" was not a little due
to the supposition that "A. B., of Phisike
Doctour," by whom the tales were said to
have been "gathered together," was none
other than Andrew Borde, or Boorde, a
Carthusian friar before the Reformation, one
of the physicians to Henry VIII., a great
traveller, even beyond the bounds of Christendom, "a thousand or two and more myles,"
a man of great learning, withal "of fame
facete." For to Borde have the *Merie Tales
of the Mad Men of Gotham* been generally
ascribed down to our own times. There is,
however, as Dr. F. J. Furnivall justly remarks,
"no good external evidence that the book

---

[1] Collier's *Bibliographical Account*, etc., vol. i.,
p. 327.

was written by Borde, while the internal
evidence is against his authorship." [1] In short,
the ascription of its compilation to "A. B., of
Phisike Doctour," was clearly a device of the
printer to sell the book. [2]

The *Tales of the Mad Men of Gotham* continued to be printed as a chap-book down
to the close of the first quarter of the present
century; and much harmless mirth they must
have caused at cottage firesides in remote
rural districts occasionally visited by the
ubiquitous pedlar, in whose well-filled pack
of all kinds of petty merchandise such drolleries were sure to be found.   Unlike other old
collections of facetiæ, the little work is re-
markably free from objectionable stories; some
are certainly not very brilliant, having, indeed,
nothing in them particularly " Gothamite,"
and one or two seem to have been adapted
from the Italian novelists.   Of the twenty
tales comprised in the collection, the first is
certainly one of the most humorous:

There were two men of Gotham, and one

[1] Forewords to Borde's *Introduction of Knowledge*, etc., edited, for the Early English Text
Society, by F. J. Furnivall.
[2] It is equally certain that Borde had no hand
either in the *Jests of Scogin* or *The Mylner of
Abyngton*, the latter an imitation of Chaucer's
Reve's Tale.

of them was going to the market at Nottingham to buy sheep, and the other was coming
from the market, and both met on Nottingham
bridge. "Well met!" said the one to the
other. "Whither are you a-going?" said he
that came from Nottingham. "Marry," said
he that was going thither, "I am going to the
market to buy sheep." "Buy sheep!" said
the other. "And which way will you bring
them home?" "Marry," said the other, "I
will bring them over this bridge." "By
Robin Hood," said he that came from
Nottingham, "but thou shalt not." "By
Maid Marian," said he that was going thither,
"but I will." "Thou shalt not," said the one.
"I will," said the other. Then they beat
their staves against the ground, one against
the other, as if there had been a hundred
sheep betwixt them. "Hold them there,"
said the one. "Beware of the leaping over
the bridge of my sheep," said the other.
"They shall all come this way," said one.
"But they shall not," said the other. And
as they were in contention, another wise man
that belonged to Gotham came from the
market, with a sack of meal upon his horse;
and seeing and hearing his neighbours at
strife about sheep, and none betwixt them,
said he, "Ah, fools, will you never learn wit?
Then help me," said he that had the meal,

"and lay this sack upon my shoulder." They did so, and he went to the one side of the bridge and unloosed the mouth of the sack, and did shake out all the meal into the river. Then said he, "How much meal is there in the sack, neighbours?" "Marry," answered they, "none." "Now, by my faith," answered this wise man, "even so much wit is there in your two heads to strive for the thing which you have not." Now which was the wisest of these three persons, I leave you to judge.

Allusions to these tales are of frequent occurrence in our literature of the sixteenth and seventeenth centuries. Dekker, in his *Gul's Horn Book* (1609), says, "It is now high time for me to have a blow at thy head, which I will not cut off with sharp documents, but rather set it on faster, bestowing upon it such excellent serving that if all the wise men of Gotham should lay their heads together, their jobbernowls should not be able to compare with thine;" and Wither, in his *Abuses*, says,

"And he that tryes to doe it might have bin
    One of the crew that hedged the cuckoo in,"

alluding to one of the most famous exploits of the wittols:

On a time the men of Gotham would have

pinned in the cuckoo, whereby she should sing all the year, and in the midst of the town they made a hedge round in compass, and they had got a cuckoo, and had put her into it, and said, " Sing here all the year, and thou shalt lack neither meat nor drink." The cuckoo, as soon as she perceived herself encompassed within the hedge, flew away. " A vengeance on her ! " said they. " We made not our hedge high enough."

The tales had, however, attained popular favour much earlier. Mr. Halliwell-Phillipps has pointed out that in *Philotimus* (1583) the men of Gotham are remembered as having " tied their rentes in a purse about an hare's necke, and bade her to carrie it to their landlord," an excellent plan, which is thus described :

On a time the men of Gotham had forgotten to pay their rent to their landlord. The one said to the other, " To-morrow is our pay-day, and what remedy shall we find to send our money to our lord ? " The one said, " This day I have taken a quick [*i.e.*, live] hare, and she shall carry it, for she is light of foot." " Be it so," said all. " She shall have a letter and a purse to put in our money, and we shall direct her the ready way." And when the letters were written, and the money put in a purse, they did tie them about the hare's neck, saying, "First thou must go to Loughborough, and then to Leicester; and at Newark there is our lord, and commend us to him, and there is his duty [*i.e.*, due]." The hare, as soon as she was out of their hands, she did run a clean contrary way. Some cried to her, saying, "Thou must go to Lough-borough first." Some said, "Let the hare alone; she can tell a nearer way than the best of us all do: let her go." Another said, "It is a noble hare; let her alone; she will not keep the highway for fear of the dogs."

The well-worn "Joe Miller" of the Irish-man who tried to count the party to which he belonged, and always forgot to count him-self, which is also known in Russia and in the West Highlands of Scotland, is simply a variant of this drollery:

On a certain day there were twelve men of Gotham that went to fish, and some stood on dry land; and in going home one said to the other, "We have ventured wonderfully in wading: I pray God that none of us come home and be drowned." "Nay, marry," said one to the other, "let us see that; for there did twelve of us come out." Then they told (*i.e.*, counted) themselves, and every one told eleven. Said one to the other, "There is one of us drowned." They went back to the brook where they had been fishing, and sought up and down for him that was wanting, making great lamentation. A courtier, coming by, asked what it was they sought for, and why they were sorrowful. "Oh," said they, "this day we went to fish in the brook twelve of us came out together, and one is drowned." Said the courtier, "Tell [count] how many there be of you." One of them said, "Eleven," and he did not tell himself. "Well," said the courtier, "what will you give me, and I will find the twelfth man?" "Sir," said they, "all the money we have got." "Give me the money," said the courtier, and began with the first, and gave him a stroke over the shoulders with his whip, which made him groan, saying, "Here is one," and so served them all, and they all groaned at the matter. When he came to the last, he paid him well, saying, "Here is the twelfth man." "God's blessing on thy heart," said they, "for thus finding our dear brother!"

This droll adventure is also found in the *Gooroo Paramartan*, a most amusing work, written in the Tamil language by Beschi, an Italian Jesuit, who was missionary in India from 1700 till his death, in 1742. The Gooroo (teacher) and his five disciples, who are, like himself, noodles, come to a river which they have to cross, and which, as the Gooroo informs them, is a very dangerous stream. To ascertain whether it is at present "asleep," one of them dips his lighted cheroot in the water, which, of course, extinguishes it, upon which he returns to the Gooroo and reports that the river is still in a dangerous mood. So they all sit down, and begin to tell stories of the destructive nature of this river. One relates how his grandfather and another man were journeying together, driving two asses laden with bags of salt, and coming to this river, they resolved to bathe in it, and the asses, tempted by the coolness of the water, at the same time knelt down in it. When the men found that their salt had disappeared, they congratulated themselves on their wonderful escape from the devouring stream, which had eaten up all their salt without even opening the bags. Another disciple relates a story similar to the so-called Æsopian fable of the dog and his shadow, this river being supposed to have devoured a piece of meat which the dog had dropped into it. At length the river is found to be quiescent, a piece of charred wood having been plunged into it without producing any effect like that of the former experiment ; and they determine to ford it, but with great caution. Arrived on the other side, they count

their number, like the men of Gotham, and
discover that one is not present. A traveller,
coming up, finds the missing man by whack-
ing each of them over the shoulder. The
Gooroo, while gratified that the lost one was
found, was grumbling at his sore bones—for
the traveller had struck pretty hard—when
an old woman, on learning of their adventure,
told them that, in her young days, she and
her female companions were once returning
home from a grand festival, and adopted
another plan for ascertaining if they were
all together. Gathering some of the cattle-
droppings, they kneaded them into a cake, in
which they each made a mark with the tip
of the nose, and then counted the marks—a
plan which the Gooroo and his disciples
should make use of on future occasions.

The Abbé Dubois has given a French
translation of the Adventures of the Gooroo
Paramartan among the *Contes Divers* appended to his not very valuable selection of
tales and apologues from Tamil, Telegu, and
Cannada versions of the *Panchatantra* (Five
Chapters, not " Cinq Ruses," as he renders
it), a Sanskrit form of the celebrated Fables
of Bidpaï, or Pilpay. An English rendering
of Beschi's work, by Babington, forms one
of the publications of the Oriental Translation Fund. Dubois states that he found

the tales of the Gooroo current in Indian
countries where Beschi's name was unknown,
and he had no doubt of their Indian origin.
However this may be, the work was probably
designed, as Babington thinks, to satirise the
Bráhmans, as well as to furnish a pleasing
vehicle of instruction to those Jesuits in
India whose duties required a knowledge
of the Tamil language.

A story akin to that of the Gothamite
fishers, if not, indeed, an older form of it,
is told in Iceland of the Three Brothers of
Bakki, who came upon one of the hot springs
which abound in that volcanic island, and
taking off their boots and stockings, put their
feet into the water and began to bathe them.
When they would rise up, they were perplexed to know each his own feet, and so
they sat disconsolate, until a wayfarer chanced
to pass by, to whom they told their case,
when he soon relieved their minds by striking
the feet of each, for which important service
they gave him many thanks.[1]   This story
reappears, slightly modified, in Campbell's
Popular Tales of the West Highlands : A
party of masons, engaged in building a dyke,
take shelter during a heavy shower, and when
it has passed, they continue sitting, because

[1] Powell and Magnusson's *Legends of Iceland,*
Second Series.

their legs had got mixed together, and none knew his own, until they were put right by a traveller with a big stick. We have here an evident relic of the Norsemen's occupation of the Hebrides.

Several of the tales of the Gothamites are found almost unaltered in Gaelic. That of the twelve fishers has been already mentioned, and here is the story of the attempt to drown an eel, which Campbell gives in similar terms in his *Tales of the West Highlands :*

When that Good Friday was come, the men of Gotham did cast their heads together what to do with their white herring, their red herring, their sprats, and salt fish. One consulted with the other, and agreed that such fish should be cast into a pond or pool (the which was in the middle of the town), that it might increase the next year ; and every man did cast them into the pool. The one said, "I have thus many white herrings ;" another said, "I have thus many sprats ;" another said, "I have thus many salt fishes; let us all go together into the pool, and we shall fare like lords the next Lent." At the beginning of next Lent the men did draw the pond, to have their fish, and there was nothing but a great eel. "Ah," said they all, "a mischief

3

on this eel, for he hath eat up all our fish!"
"What shall we do with him?" said the one to
hte other. "Kill him!" said one of them.
"Chop him all to pieces!" said another.
"Nay, not so," said the other; "let us drown
him." "Be it so," said all. They went to
another pool, and did cast the eel into the
water. "Lie there," said they, "and shift for
thyself, for no help thou shalt have of us;"
and there they left the eel to be drowned.

Campbell's Gaelic story differs so little
from the above that we must suppose it to
have been derived directly from the English
chap-book. Oral tradition always produces
local variations from a written story, of which
we have an example in a Gaelic version of
this choice exploit:

There was a man of Gotham who went to
the market of Nottingham to sell cheese; and
as he was going down the hill to Nottingham
Bridge, one of his cheeses fell out of his
wallet and ran down the hill. "Ah," said the
fellow, "can you run to the market alone? I
will now send one after the other;" then laying
down the wallet and taking out the cheeses,
he tumbled them down the hill one after the
other; and some ran into one bush, and some
into another; so at last he said, "I do
charge you to meet me in the market-place."

And when the man came into the market to meet the cheeses, he stayed until the market was almost done, then went and inquired of his neighbours and other men if they did see his cheeses come to market. "Why, who should bring them?" said one of the neighbours. "Marry, themselves," said the fellow; "they knew the way well enough," said he: "a vengeance on them! For I was afraid to see my cheeses run so fast, that they would run beyond the market. I am persuaded that they are at this time almost as far as York." So he immediately takes a horse and rides after them to York; but to this day no man has ever heard of the cheeses.

In one Gaelic variant a woman is going to Inverness with a basket filled with balls of worsted of her own spinning, and going down a hill, one of the balls tumbles out and rolls along briskly, upon which she sends the others after it, holding the ends of each in her hand; and when she reaches the town, she finds a "ravelled bank" instead of her neat balls of worsted. In another version a man goes to market with two bags of cheese, and sends them downhill, like the Gothamite. After waiting at the market all day in vain, he returns home, and tells his wife of his misfortune. She goes to the foot of the hill and finds all the cheese.

The next Gothamite tale also finds its counterpart in the Gaelic stories: There was a man of Gotham who bought at Nottingham a trivet, or brandiron, and as he was going home his shoulders grew sore with the carriage thereof, and he set it down; and seeing that it had three feet, he said, "Ha! hast thou three feet, and I but two? Thou shalt bear me home, if thou wilt," and set himself down thereupon, and said to the trivet, "Bear me as long as I have borne thee; but if thou do not, thou shalt stand still for me." The man of Gotham did see that his trivet would not go farther. "Stand still, in the mayor's name," said he, "and follow me if thou wilt. I will tell thee right the way to my home." When he did come to his house, his wife said, "Where is my trivet?" The man said, "He hath three legs, and I have but two; and I did teach him the way to my house. Let him come home if he will." "Where left ye the trivet?" said the woman. "At Gotham hill," said the man. His wife did run and fetch home the trivet her own self, or else she had lost it through her husband's wit.

In Campbell's version a man having been sent by his wife with her spinning-wheel to get mended, as he was returning home with it the wind set the wheel in motion, so he put it down, and bidding it go straight to his house, set off himself. When he reached home, he asked his wife if the spinning-wheel had arrived yet, and on her replying that it had not, "I thought as much," quoth he, "for I took the shorter way."

A somewhat similar story is found in Rivière's French collection of tales of the Kabaïl, Algeria, to this effect : The mother of a youth of the Beni-Jennad clan gave him a hundred reals to buy a mule ; so he went to market, and on his way met a man carrying a water-melon for sale. "How much for the melon?" he asks. "What will you give?" says the man. "I have only got a hundred reals," answered the booby ; "had I more, you should have it." "Well," rejoined the man, "I'll take them." Then the youth took the melon and handed over the money. "But tell me," says he, "will its young one be as green as it is?" "Doubtless," answered the man, "it will be green." As the booby was going home, he allowed the melon to roll down a slope before him. It burst on its way, when up started a frightened hare. "Go to my house, young one," he shouted. "Surely a green animal has come out of it." And when he got home, he inquired of his mother if the young one had arrived.

In the *Gooroo Paramartan* there is a parallel incident to this last. The noodles are desirous of providing their Gooroo with a horse, and a man sells them a pumpkin, telling them it is a mare's egg, which only requires to be sat upon for a certain time to produce a fine young horse. The Gooroo himself undertakes to hatch the mare's egg, since his disciples have all other matters to attend to; but as they are carrying it through a jungle, it falls down and splits into pieces; just then a frightened hare runs before them; and they inform the Gooroo that a fine young colt came out of the mare's egg, with very long ears, and ran off with the speed of the wind. It would have proved a fine horse for their revered Gooroo, they add; but he consoles himself for the loss by reflecting that such an animal would probably have run away with him.

A number of the Gothamite tales in the printed collection are not only inferior to those which are preserved orally, but can be considered in no sense examples of preeminent folly. Three consist of tricks played by women upon their husbands, such as are found in the ordinary jest-books of the sixteenth and seventeenth centuries. In one a man, who had taken a buzzard, invites some friends to dine with him. His wife, with two of her gossips, having secretly eaten the buzzard,

kills and cooks an old goose, and sets it
before him and his guests; the latter call him
a knave to mock them thus with an old goose,
and go off in great anger. The husband,
resolved to put himself right with his friends,
stuffs the buzzard's feathers into a sack, in
order to show them that they were mistaken
in thinking he had tried to deceive them with
an old goose instead of a fine fat buzzard.
But before he started on this business, his
wife contrived to substitute the goose's
feathers, which he exhibited to his friends as
those of the buzzard, and was soundly cudgelled for what they believed to be a second
attempt to mock them.— Two other stories
seem to be derived from the Italian novelists:
of the man who intended cutting off his wife's
hair[1] and of the man who defied his wife to
cuckold him. Two others turn upon wrong
responses at a christening and a marriage,
which have certainly nothing Gothamite in
them. Another is a dull story of a Scotchman
who employed a carver to make him as a
sign of his inn a boar's head, the tradesman
supposing from his northern pronunciation

[1] An imitation of Boccaccio, *Decameron*, Day
vii., nov. 8, who perhaps borrowed the story from
Guérin's *fabliau* " De la Dame qui fit accroire à
son Mari qu'il avait rêvé ; *aliàs*, Les Cheveux
Coupés " (Le Grand's *Fabliaux*, ed. 1781, tome
ii., 280).

that he meant a *bare* head.—In the nine-
teenth tale, a party of gossips are assembled
at the alehouse, and each relates in what
manner she is profitable to her husband : one
saves candles by sending all her household
to bed in daylight; another, like the old
fellow and Tib his wife in *Jolly Good Ale
and Old,* eats little meat, but can swig a
gallon or two of ale, and so forth.

We have, however, our Gothamite once
more in the story of him who, seeing a fine
cheese on the ground as he rode along the
highway, tried to pick it up with his sword,
and finding his sword too short, rode back to
fetch a longer one for his purpose, but when
he returned, he found the cheese was gone. "A
murrain take it!" quoth he. "If I had had this
sword, I had had this cheese myself, and now
another hath got it!" Also in the smith who
took a red-hot iron bar and thrust it into the
thatch of his smithy to destroy a colony of
wasps, and, of course, burned down the
smithy—a story which has done duty in
modern days to "point a moral" in the form
of a teetotal tract, with a drunken smith in
place of the honest Gothamite![1]

---

[1] A slightly different version occurs in the
Tale of Beryn, which is found in a unique MS. of
Chaucer's *Canterbury Tales,* and which forms
the first part of the old French romance of the

The following properly belongs to stories of the "silly son" class: There was a young man of Gotham the which should go wooing to a fair maid. His mother did warn him beforehand, saying, "When thou dost look upon her, cast a sheep's-eye, and say, 'How do ye, sweet pigsnie?'" The fellow went to the butcher's and bought seven or eight sheep's eyes; and when this lusty wooer did sit at dinner, he would cast in her face a sheep's eye, saying, "How dost thou, my pretty pigsnie?" "How do I?" said the wench. "Swine's-face, why dost thou cast the sheep's eye upon me?" "O sweet pigsnie, have at thee another!" "I defy thee, Swine's-face," said the wench. The fellow, being abashed, said, "What, sweet pigsnie! Be content, for if thou do live until the next year, thou wilt be a foul sow." "Walk, knave, walk!" said she; "for if thou live till the

Chevalier Berinus. In the English poem Beryn, lamenting his misfortunes, and that he had disinherited himself, says:

"But I fare like the man, that for to swale his vlyes
    [*i.e.* flies]
He stert in-to the bern, and aftir stre he hies,
And goith a-bout with a brennyng wase,
Tyll it was atte last that the leam and blase
Entryd in-to the chynys, wher the whete was,
And kissid so the evese, that brent was al the plase."

It is certain that the author of the French original of the *Tale of Beryn* did not get this tory out of our jests of the men of Gotham.

next year, thou wilt be a stark knave, a lubber, and a fool."

It is very evident that the men of Gotham were of "honest" Jack Falstaff's opinion that the better part of valour is discretion: On a time there was a man of Gotham a-mowing in the meads and found a great grasshopper. He cast down his scythe, and did run home to his neighbours, and said that there was a devil in the field that hopped in the grass. Then there was every man ready with clubs and staves, with halberts, and with other weapons, to go and kill the grasshopper. When they did come to the place where the grasshopper should be, said the one to the other, "Let every man cross himself from the devil, or we will not meddle with him." And so they returned again, and said, "We were all blessed this day that we went no farther." "Ah, cowards," said he that had his scythe in the mead, "help me to fetch my scythe." "No," said they; "it is good to sleep in a whole skin: better it is to lose thy scythe than to mar us all."

There is some spice of humour in the concluding tale of the printed collection, although it has no business there: On Ash Wednesday the priest said to the men of Gotham, "If I should enjoin you to prayer, there is none of you that can say your paternoster;

and you be now too old to learn. And to enjoin you to fast were foolishness, for you do not eat a good meal's meat in a year. Wherefore do I enjoin thee to labour all the week, that thou mayest fare well to dine on Sunday, and I will come to dinner and see it to be so, and take my dinner." Another man he did enjoin to fare well on Monday, and another on Tuesday, and one after another that one or other should fare well once a week, that he might have part of his meat. "And as for alms," said the priest, "ye be beggars all, except one or two; therefore bestow alms on yourselves."

Among the numerous stories of the Gothamites preserved orally, but not found in the collection of "A. B., of Phisicke Doctour," is the following, which seems to be of Indian extraction:

One day some men of Gotham were walking by the riverside, and came to a place where the contrary currents caused the water to boil as in a whirlpool. "See how the water boils!" says one. "If we had plenty of oatmeal," says another, "we might make enough porridge to serve all the village for a month." So it was resolved that part of them should go to the village and fetch their oatmeal, which was soon brought and thrown into the river. But there presently arose the question of how they were to know when the porridge was ready. This difficulty was overcome by the offer of one of the company to jump in, and it was agreed that if he found it ready for use, he should signify the same to his companions. The man jumped in, and found the water deeper than he expected. Thrice he rose to the surface, but said nothing. The others, impatient at his remaining so long silent, and seeing him smack his lips, took this for an avowal that the porridge was good, and so they all jumped in after him and were drowned.

Another traditional Gothamite story is related of a villager coming home at a late hour, and, seeing the reflection of the moon in a horse-pond, believed it to be a green cheese, and roused all his neighbours to help him to draw it out. They raked and raked away until a passing cloud sank the cheese, when they returned to their homes grievously disappointed.[1] — This is also related of the

---

[1] There is an analogous Indian story of a youth who went to a tank to drink, and observing the reflection of a golden-crested bird that was sitting on a tree, he thought it was gold in the water, and entered the tank to take it up, but he could not lay hold of it as it appeared and disappeared in the water. But as often as he ascended the bank he again saw it in the water

villagers near the Marlborough Downs, in Wiltshire, and the *sobriquet* of "moon-rakers," applied to Wiltshire folk in general, is said to have had its origin in the incident ; but they assert that it was a keg of smuggled brandy, which had been sunk in a pond, that the villagers were attempting to fish up, when the exciseman coming suddenly upon the scene, they made him believe they were raking the reflection of the moon, thinking it a green cheese, an explanation which is on

and again he entered the tank to lay hold of it, and still he got nothing. At length his father saw and questioned him, then drove away the bird, and explaining the matter to him, took the foolish fellow home.

We have already seen that the men of Abdera (p. 5) flogged an ass before its fellows for upsetting a jar of olive oil, but what is that compared with the story of the ass that drank up the moon ? According to Ludovicus Vives, a learned Spanish writer, certain townspeople imprisoned an ass for drinking up the moon, whose reflection, appearing in the water, was covered with a cloud while the ass was drinking. Next day the poor beast was brought to the bar to be sentenced according to his deserts. After the grave burghers had discussed the affair for some time, one at length rose up and declared that it was not fit the town should lose its moon, but rather that the ass should be cut open and the moon he had swallowed taken out of him, which, being cordially approved by the others, was done accordingly.

a par with the apocryphal tale of the Gothamites and the messengers of King John.

The absurd notion of the moon being a fine
cheese is of very respectable antiquity, and
occurs in the noodle-stories of many countries.
It is referred to by Rabelais, and was doubtless the subject of a popular French tale in
his time. In the twenty-second story of the
Disciplina Clericalis of Peter Alfonsus, a
Spanish Jew, who was baptised in 1106,
a fox leaves a wolf in a well, looking after a
supposed cheese, made by the image of the
moon in the water; and the same fable had
been told by the Talmudists in the fifth century.[1] The well-known "Joe Miller" of the
party of Irishmen who endeavoured to reach
a "green cheese" in the river by hanging one
by another's legs finds its parallel in a Meck-
lenburg story, in which some men by the
same contrivance tried to get a stone from the
bottom of a well, and the incident is thus
related in the old English jest-book entitled
The Sacke Full of Newes:

There were three young men going to Lam-
beth along by the waterside, and one played
with the other, and they cast each other's caps
into the water in such sort as they could not
get their caps again. But over the place

[1] This is also one of the Fables of Marie de
France (thirteenth century).

where their caps were did grow a great old tree, the which did cover a great deal of the water. One of them said to the rest, " Sirs, I have found a notable way to come by them. First I will make myself fast by the middle with one of your girdles unto the tree, and he that is with you shall hang fast upon my girdle, and he that is last shall take hold on him that holds fast on my girdle, and so with one of his hands he may take up all our caps, and cast them on the sand." And so they did ; but when they thought that they had been most secure and fast, he that was above felt his girdle slack, and said, " Soft, sirs ! My girdle slacketh." " Make it fast quickly," said they. But as he was untying it to make it faster they fell all three into the water, and were well washed for their pains.

Closely allied to these tales is the Russian story of the old man who planted a cabbage-head in the cellar, under the floor of his cottage, and, strange to say, it grew right up to the sky. He climbs up the cabbage-stalk till he reaches the sky. There he sees a mill, which gives a turn, and out come a pie and a cake, with a pot of stewed grain on the top. The old man eats his fill and drinks his fill ; then he lies down to sleep. By-and-bye he awakes, and slides down to earth again.

He tells his wife of the good things up in the sky, and she induces him to take her with him. She slips into a sack, and the old man takes it in his teeth and begins to climb up. The old woman, becoming tired, asked him if it was much farther, and just as he was about to say, " Not much farther," the sack slipped from between his teeth, and the old woman fell to the ground and was smashed to pieces.

There are many variants of this last story (which is found in Mr. Ralston's most valuable and entertaining collection of Russian folk-tales), but observe the very close resemblance which it bears to the following Indian tale of the fools and the bull of Siva, from the *Kathá Sarit Ságara* (Ocean of the Streams of Story), the grand collection, composed in Sanskrit verse by Somadeva in the eleventh century, from a similar work entitled *Vrihat Kathá* (Great Story), written in Sanskrit prose by Gunadhya, in the sixth century : [1]

In a certain convent, which was full of fools, there was a man who was the greatest

[1] A complete translation of the *Kathá Sarit Ságara*, by Professor C. H. Tawney, with notes of variants, which exhibit his wide acquaintance with the popular fictions of all lands, has been recently published at Calcutta (London agents, Messrs. Trübner and Co.), a work which must prove invaluable to every English student of comparative folk-lore.

fool of the lot. He once heard in a treatise on law, which was being read aloud, that a man who has a tank made gains a great reward in the next world. Then, as he had a large fortune, he had made a large tank full of water, at no great distance from his own convent. One day this prince of fools went to take a look at that tank of his, and perceived that the sand had been scratched up by some creature. The next day too he came, and saw that the bank had been torn up in another part of the tank, and being quite astonished, he said to himself, "I will watch here to-morrow the whole day, beginning in the early morning, and I will find out what creature it is that does this." After he had formed this resolution, he came there early next morning, and watched, until at last he saw a bull descend from heaven and plough up the bank with its horns, He thought, "This is a heavenly bull, so why should I not go to heaven with it?" And he went up to the bull, and with both his hands laid hold of the tail behind. Then the holy bull lifted up, with the utmost force, the foolish man who was clinging to its tail, and carried him in a moment to its home in Kailása.[1] There

[1] Siva's paradise, according to Hindú mythology, is on Mount Kailása, in the Himályas, north of Mánasa.

the foolish man lived for some time in great comfort, feasting on heavenly dainties, sweetmeats, and other things which he obtained. And seeing that the bull kept going and returning, that king of fools, bewildered by destiny, thought, "I will go down clinging to the tail of the bull and see my friends, and after I have told them this wonderful tale, I will return in the same way." Having formed this resolution, the fool went and clung to the tail of the bull one day when it was setting out, and so returned to the surface of the earth. When he entered the convent, the other blockheads who were there embraced him, and asked him where he had been, and he told them. Then all these foolish men, having heard the tale of his adventures, made this petition to him: "Be kind, and take us also there; enable us also to feast on sweetmeats." He consented, and told them his plan for doing it, and next day led them to the border of the tank, and the bull came there. And the principal fool seized the tail of the bull with his two hands, and another took hold of his feet, and a third in turn took hold of his. So, when they had formed a chain by hanging on to one another's feet, the bull flew rapidly up into the air. And while the bull was going along, with all the fools clinging to its tail, it happened that one

of the fools said to the principal fool, "Tell
us now, to satisfy our curiosity, how large
were the sweetmeats which you ate, of which
a never-failing supply can be obtained in
heaven?" Then the leader had his attention
diverted from the business in hand, and
quickly joined his hands together like the cup
of a lotus, and exclaimed in answer, "So
big." But in so doing he let go the tail of the
bull, and accordingly he and all those others
fell from heaven, and were killed; and the
bull returned to Kailása; but the people who
saw it were much amused.[1]

"Thus," remarks the story-teller, "fools do
themselves injury by asking questions and
giving answers without reflection"; he then
proceeds to relate a story in illustration of
the apothegm that "association with fools
brings prosperity to no man":

A certain fool, while going to another
village, forgot the way. And when he asked
the way, the people said to him, "Take the
path that goes up by the tree on the bank of
the river." Then the fool went and got on
the trunk of that tree, and said to himself,
"The men told me that my way lay up the
trunk of this tree." And as he went on
climbing up it, the bough at the end bent

[1] Tawney's translation, which is used throughout this work.

with his weight, and it was all he could do to avoid falling by clinging to it. While he was clinging to it, there came that way an elephant that had been drinking water, with his driver on his back. And the fool called to him, saying, "Great sir, take me down." The elephant-driver laid hold of him by the feet with both his hands, to take him down from the tree. Meanwhile the elephant went on, and the driver found himself clinging to the feet of the fool, who was clinging to the end of the tree. Then said the fool to the driver, "Sing something, in order that the people may hear, and come at once and take us down." So the elephant-driver, thus appealed to, began to sing, and he sang so sweetly that the fool was much pleased; and in his desire to applaud him, he forgot what he was about, let go his hold of the tree, and prepared to clap him with both his hands; and immediately he and the elephant-driver fell into the river and were drowned.

The germ of all stories of this class is perhaps found in the *Játakas,* or Buddhist Birth Stories: A pair of geese resolve to migrate to another country, and agree to carry with them a tortoise, their intimate friend, taking the ends of a stick between their bills, and the tortoise grasping it by the middle with his mouth. As they are flying over

Bánáres, the people exclaim in wonder to one another at such a strange sight, and the tortoise, unable to maintain silence, opens his mouth to rebuke them, and by so doing falls to the ground, and is dashed into pieces. This fable is also found in Babrius (115); in the *Kathá Sarit Ságara*, in the several versions of the Fables of Bidpaï; and in the *Avadánas*, translated into French from the Chinese by Stanislas Julien.

To return to Gothamite stories. According to one of those which are current orally, the men of Gotham had but one knife among them, which was stuck in a tree in the middle of the village for their common use, and many amusing incidents, says Mr. Halliwell-Phillipps, arose out of their disputes for the use of this knife. The " carles " of Austwick, in Yorkshire, are said also to have had but one knife, or "whittle," which was deposited under a tree, and if it was not found there when wanted, the " carle " requiring it called out, "Whittle to the tree!" This plan did very well for some years, until it was taken one day by a party of labourers to a neighbouring moor, to be used for cutting their bread and cheese. When the day's labour was done, they resolved to leave the knife at the place,

to save themselves the trouble of carrying it
back, as they should want it again next day;
so they looked about for some object to mark
the spot, and stuck it into the ground under a
black cloud that happened to be the most
remarkable object in sight.   But next day,
when they returned to the place, the cloud was
gone, and the " whittle " was never seen again.

When an Austwick " carle " comes into
any of the larger towns of Yorkshire, it is
said he is greeted with the question, " Who
tried to lift the bull over the gate ? " in allu-
sion to the following story: An Austwick
farmer, wishing to get a bull out of a field—
how the animal got into it, the story does not
inform us—procured the assistance of nine of
his neighbours to lift the animal over the gate.
After trying in vain for some hours, they sent
one of their number to the village for more
help.   In going out he opened the gate, and
after he had gone away, it occurred to one of
those who remained that the bull might be·
allowed to go out in the same manner.

Another Austwick farmer had to take a
wheelbarrow to a certain town, and, to save
a hundred yards by going the ordinary road,
he went through the fields, and had to lift the
barrow over twenty-two stiles.

It was a Wiltshire man, however (if all
tales be true), who determined to cure the

filthy habits of his hogs by making them roost upon the branches of a tree, like birds. Night after night the pigs were hoisted up to their perch, and every morning one of them was found with its neck broken, until at last there were none left.—And quite as witless, surely, was the device of the men of Belmont, who once desired to move their church three yards farther westward, so they carefully marked the exact distance by leaving their coats on the ground. Then they set to work to push with all their might against the eastern wall. In the meantime a thief had gone round to the west side and stolen their coats. "Diable!" exclaimed they on finding that their coats were gone, "we have pushed too far!"

CHAPTER III.

HE Schildburgers, it has been already remarked, are the Gothamites of Germany, and the stories of their stupidity, after being orally current for years among the people, were collected near the close of the sixteenth century, the earliest known edition being that of 1597. In a most lively and entertaining article on "Early German Comic Romances" (*Foreign Quarterly Review*, No. 40, 1837), the late Mr. W. J. Thoms has furnished an account of the exploits of the Schildburgers, from which the following particulars and tales are extracted: "There have been few happier ideas than that of making these simpletons descend from one of the wise men of Greece, and representing them as originally gifted with such extraordinary talents as to be called to the councils of all the princes of the earth, to the great detriment of their circumstances and the still greater dissatisfaction of their

wives, and then, upon their being summoned home to arrange their disordered affairs, determining, in their wisdom, to put on the garb of stupidity, and persevering so long and so steadfastly in their assumed character as to prove 'plain fools at last.' No way inferior is the end of this strange tale, which assumes even somewhat of serious interest when the Schildburgers, after performing every conceivable piece of folly, and receiving the especial privilege of so doing under the seal and signature of the emperor, by the crowning act of their lives turn themselves out of house and home, whereby they are compelled, like the Jews, to become outcasts and wanderers over the face of the earth, by which means it has arisen that there is no spot, however remote, on which some of their descendants, who may be known by their characteristic stupidity, are not to be found."

Their first piece of folly was to build a council-house without windows. When they entered it, and, to use the words of the nursery ballad, "saw they could not see," they were greatly puzzled to account for such a state of things; and having in vain gone outside and examined the building to find why the inside was dark, they determined to hold a council upon the subject on the following day. At the time appointed they assembled, each bringing with him a torch, which, on seating himself, he stuck in his hat. After much discussion, one genius, brighter than the rest, decided that they could not see for want of daylight, and that they ought on the morrow to carry in as much of it as possible. Accordingly, the next day, when the sun shone, all the sacks, bags, boxes, baskets, tubs, pans, etc. of the village were filled with its beams and carefully carried into the council-house and emptied there, but with no good effect. After this they removed the roof, by the advice of a traveller, whom they rewarded amply for the suggestion. This plan answered famously during the summer, but when the rains of winter fell, and they were forced to replace the roof, they found the house just as dark as ever. Again they met, again they stuck their torches in their hats, but to no purpose, until by chance one of them was quitting the house, and groping his way along the wall, when a ray of light fell through a crevice and upon his beard, whereupon he suggested, what had never occurred to any of them, that it was possible they might get daylight in by making a window.

Another tale relates how the boors of Schilda contrived to get their millstone twice down from a high mountain :

The boors of Schilda had built a mill, and with extraordinary labour they had quarried a millstone for it out of a quarry which lay on the summit of a high mountain ; and when the stone was finished, they carried it with great labour and pain down the hill. When they had got to the bottom, it occurred to one of them that they might have spared themselves the trouble of carrying it down by letting it roll down. "Verily," said he, "we are the stupidest of fools to take these extraordinary pains to do that which we might have done with so little trouble. We will carry it up, and then let it roll down the hill by itself, as we did before with the tree which we felled for the council-house."

This advice pleased them all, and with greater labour they carried the stone to the top of the mountain again, and were about to roll it down, when one of them said, "But how shall we know where it runs to ? Who will be able to tell us aught about it ?" "Why," said the bailiff, who had advised the stone being carried up again, "this is very easily managed. One of us must stick in the hole [for the millstone, of course, had a hole in the middle], and run down with it."

This was agreed to, and one of them, having
been chosen for the purpose, thrust his head
through the hole, and ran down the hill with
the millstone. Now at the bottom of the
mountain was a deep fish-pond, into which
the stone rolled, and the simpleton with it,
so that the Schildburgers lost both stone and
man, and not one among them knew what
had become of them. And they felt sorely
angered against their old companion who had
run down the hill with the stone, for they
considered that he had carried it off for the
purpose of disposing of it. So they published
a notice in all the neighbouring boroughs,
towns, and villages, calling on them, that "it
any one come there with a millstone round
his neck, they should treat him as one who
had stolen the common goods, and give him
to justice." But the poor fellow lay in the
pond, dead. Had he been able to speak, he
would have been willing to tell them not to
worry themselves on his account, for he would
give them their own again. But his load
pressed so heavily upon him, and he was so
deep in the water, that he, after drinking
water enough—more, indeed, than was good
for him—died; and he is dead at the present
day, and dead he will, shall, and must
remain !

The forty-seventh chapter recounts "How the Schildburgers purchased a mouser, and with it their own ruin":

Now it happened that there were no cats in Schilda, and so many mice that nothing was safe, even in the bread-basket, for whatsoever they put there was sure to be gnawed or eaten; and this grieved them sorely. And upon a time there came a traveller into the village, carrying a cat in his arms, and he entered the hostel. The host asked him, "What sort of a beast is that?" Said he, "It is a mouser." Now the mice at Schilda were so quiet and so tame that they never fled before the people, but ran about all day long, without the slightest fear. So the traveller let the cat run, who, in the sight of the host, soon caught numbers of mice. Now when the people were told this by the host, they asked the man whether the mouser was to be sold, for they would pay him well for it. He said, "It certainly was not to be sold; but seeing that it would be so useful to them, he would let them have it if they would pay him what was right," and he asked a hundred florins for it. The boors were glad to find that he asked so little, and concluded a bargain with him, he agreeing to take half the money down, and to come again in six months to fetch the rest. As soon as the bargain was struck on both sides, they gave the traveller the half of the money, and he carried the mouser into the granary, where they kept their corn, for there were most mice there. The traveller went off with the money at full speed, for he feared greatly lest they should repent them of the bargain, and want their money back again; and as he went along he kept looking behind him to see that no one was following him. Now the boors had forgotten to ask what the cat was to be fed upon, so they sent one after him in haste to ask him the question. But when he with the gold saw that some one was following him, he hastened so much the more, so that the boor could by no means overtake him, whereupon he called out to him from afar off, "What does it eat?" "What you please! What you please!" quoth the traveller. But the peasant understood him to say, "Men and beasts! Men and beasts!" Therefore he returned home in great affliction, and said as much to his worthy masters.

On learning this they became greatly alarmed, and said, "When it has no more mice to eat, it will eat our cattle; and when they are gone, it will eat us! To think that we should lay out our good money in buying such a thing!" And they held counsel together and resolved that the cat should be killed.

But no one would venture to lay hold of it for that purpose, whereupon it was determined to burn the granary, and the cat in it, seeing that it was better they should suffer a common loss than all lose life and limb. So they set fire to the granary. But when the cat smelt the fire, it sprang out of a window and fled to another house, and the granary was burned to the ground. Never was there sorrow greater than that of the Schildburgers when they found that they could not kill the cat. They counselled with one another, and purchased the house to which the cat had fled, and burned that also. But the cat sprang out upon the roof, and sat there, washing itself and putting its paws behind its ears, after the manner of cats; and the Schildburgers understood thereby that the cat lifted up its hands and swore an oath that it would not leave their treatment of it unrevenged. Then one of them took a long pole and struck at the cat, but the cat caught hold of the pole, and began to clamber down it, whereupon all the people grew greatly alarmed and ran away, and left the fire to burn as it might. And because no one regarded the fire, nor sought to put it out, the whole village was burned to a house, and notwithstanding that, the cat escaped. And the Schildburgers fled with their wives and children to a neighbouring forest. And at this time was burned their chancery and all the papers therein, which is the reason why their history is not to be found described in a more regular manner.

Thus ended the career of the Schild-burgers as a community, according to the veracious chronicle of their marvellous exploits, the first of which, their carrying sunshine into the council-house, is a favourite incident in the noodle-stories of many countries, and has its parallel in the Icelandic story of the Three Brothers of Bakki: They had observed that in winter the weather was colder than in summer, also that the larger the windows of a house were the colder it was. All frost and sharp cold, therefore, they thought sprang from the fact that houses had windows in them. So they built themselves a house on a new plan, without windows in it at all. It followed, of course, that there was always pitch darkness in it. They found that this was rather a fault in the house, but comforted themselves with the certainty that in winter it would be very warm; and as to light, they thought they could contrive some easy means of getting the house lighted. One fine day in the middle of summer, when the sunshine was brightest, they began to carry the darkness out of the house in their caps, and emptied it out when they came into the sunshine, which they then carried into the dark room. Thus they worked hard the whole day, but in the evening, when they had done all their best, they were not a little disappointed to find that it was as dark as before, so much so that they could not tell one hand from the other.[1]

There is a Kashmír story which bears a slight resemblance to the exploit of the Schildburgers with the cat. A poor old woman used to beg her food by day and cook it at night. Half of the food she would eat in the morning, and the other half in the evening. After a while a cat got to know of this arrangement, and came and ate the meal for her. The old woman was very patient, but at last could no longer endure the cat's impudence, and so she laid hold of it. She argued with herself as to whether she should kill it or not. "If I slay it," she thought, "it will be a sin; but if I keep it alive, it will be to my heavy loss." So she determined only to punish it. She procured some cotton wool and some oil, and soaking the one in the other, tied it on to the cat's tail and then set it on fire. Away rushed the cat across the yard, up the side of the

[1] Powell and Magnusson's *Legends of Iceland,* Second Series, p. 626.

5

window, and on to the roof, where its flaming tail ignited the thatch and set the whole house on fire. The flames soon spread to other houses, and the whole village was destroyed.[1]

An older form of this incident is found in the introduction to a Persian poetical version of the Book of Sindibád (*Sindibád Náma*), of which a unique MS. copy, very finely illuminated, but imperfect, is preserved in the Library of the India Office:[2] In a village called Buzina-Gird (*i.e.*, Monkey Town) there was a goat that was in the habit of butting at a certain old woman whenever she came into the street. One day the old woman had been to ask fire from a neighbour, and on her return the goat struck her so violently with his horns when she was off her guard as to draw blood. Enraged at this, she applied the fire which she held to the goat's fleece, which kindled, and the animal ran to the stables of the elephant-keeper, and rubbed his sides against the reeds and willows. They caught fire, which the wind soon spread, and the heads and faces of the warlike elephants were

[1] *Dictionary of Kashmiri Proverbs and Sayings.* Explained and illustrated from the rich and interesting folk-lore of the Valley. By the Rev. J. Hinton Knowles. Bombay: 1885.

[2] This work was composed A.H. 776 (A.D. 1374-5), as the anonymous author takes care to inform us in his opening verses.

scorched. With the sequel—how the king caused all the monkeys to be slaughtered, as their fat was required to cure the scorched elephants—we have no concern at present.[1]

In Ceylon whole districts, such as Tumpane, in the central province, Morora Korle, in the southern province, and Rayigam Korle, in the western province, are credited with being the abode of fools. A learned writer on the proverbial sayings of the Sinhalese states that these often refer to " popular stories of stupid people to which foolish actions are likened. The stories of the Tumpane villagers who tried to unearth and carry off a well because they saw a bees' nest reflected in the water ; of the Morora Korle boatmen who mistook a bend in the river for the sea, left their cargo there, and returned home ; of the Rayigam Korle fools who threw

[1] A still older form of the story occurs in the *Pancha Tantra* (Five Sections), a Sanskrit version of the celebrated Fables of Bidpai, in which a gluttonous ram is in the habit of going to the king's kitchen and devouring all food within his reach. One of the cooks beat him with a burning log of wood, and the ram rushed off with his blazing fleece and set the horses' stables on fire, and so forth. The story is most probably of Buddhist extraction.

stones at the moon to frighten her off one
fine moonlight night when they thought she
was coming too near, and that there was dan-
ger of her burning their crops, are well known,
and it is customary to ask a man if he was
born in one of these places if he has done
anything particularly foolish. The story of
the double-fool—*i.e.,* of the man who tried to
lighten the boat by carrying his pingo load
over his shoulders ;[1] of the man who stretched
out his hands to be warmed by the fire on the
other side of the river ; of the rustic's wife
who had her own head shaved, so as not to
lose the barber's services for the day when he
came, and her husband was away from home ;
of the villagers who tied up their mortars in
the village in the belief that the elephant
tracks in the rice fields were caused by the
mortars wandering about at night ; of the man
who would not wash his body in order to
spite the river ; of the people who flogged the
elk-skin at home to avenge themselves on the
deer that trespassed in the fields at night ;
and of the man who performed the five precepts—all these are popular stories of foolish
people which have passed into proverbs."[2]

[1] A Sinhalese variant of the exploit of the man
of Norfolk and of the man of Gotham with the
sack of meal. See *ante,* p. 19.

[2] Mr. C. J. R. le Mesurier in *The Orientalist*
(Kandy, Ceylon : 1884), pp. 233-4.

The last of the stories referred to in the above extract is as follows: A woman once rebuked her husband for not performing the five (Buddhist) precepts. "I don't know what they are," he replied. "Oh, it's very easy," she said; "all you have to do is to go to the priest and repeat what he says after him." "Is that all?" he answered. "Then I'll go and do it at once." Off he went, and as he neared the temple the priest saw him and called out, "Who are you?" to which he replied, "Who are you?" "What do you want?" demands the priest. "What do you want?" the blockhead answers dutifully. "Are you mad?" roared the priest. "Are you mad?" returned the rustic. "Here," said the priest to his attendants, "take and beat him well;" and notwithstanding that he carefully repeated the words again, taken and thoroughly well thrashed he was, after which he crawled back to his wife and said, "What a wonderful woman you are! You manage to repeat the five precepts every day, and are strong and healthy, while I, who have only said them once, am nearly dead with fever from the bruises." [1]

To this last may be added a story in the

[1] *The Orientalist,* 1884, p. 234. A much fuller version, with subsequent incidents, is given in the same excellent periodical, pp. 36—38

Kathá Manjari, a Canarese collection, of
the stupid fellow and the *Rámáyana*, one of
the two great Hindû epics: One day a man
was reading the *Rámáyana* in the bazaar, and
a woman, thinking her husband might be instructed by hearing it, sent him there. He
went, and stood leaning on his crook—for he
was a shepherd—when presently a practical
joker, seeing his simplicity, jumped upon his
shoulders, and he stood with the man on his
back until the discourse was concluded.
When he reached home, his wife asked him
how he liked the *Rámáyana*. "Alas!" said
he, "it was not easy; it was a man's load."

The race of Gothamites is indeed found
everywhere—in popular tales, if not in actual
life; and their sayings and doings are not less
diverting when husband and wife are well
mated, as in the following story:

An Arab observing one morning that his
house was ready to tumble about his ears
from decay, and being without the means of
repairing it, went with a long face to his wife,
and informed her of his trouble. She said,
"Why, my dear, need you distress yourself
about so small a matter? You have a cow
worth thirty dirhams; take her to the market
and sell her for that sum. I have some

thread, which I will dispose of to-day, and I warrant you that between us both we shall manage very well." The man at once drove the cow to the market, and gave her over for sale to the appraiser of cattle. The salesman showed her to the bystanders, directed their attention to all her good points, expatiated on all her good qualities, and, in short, passed her off as a cow of inestimable value. To all this the simpleton listened with delight and astonishment; he heard his cow praised for qualities that no other cow ever possessed, and determined in his own mind not to lose so rare a bargain, but purchase her himself and balk the chapmen. He therefore called out to the appraiser, and asked him what she was going at. The salesman replied, " At fifteen dirhams and upwards." " By the head of the Prophet," exclaimed the wittol, "had I known that my cow was such a prodigy of excellence, you should not have caught me in the market with her for sale." Now it happened that he had just fifteen dirhams, and no more, and these he thrust upon the broker, exclaiming, " The cow is mine; I have the best claim to her." He then seized the cow and drove her home, exulting all the way as if he had found a treasure. On reaching home he inquired eagerly for his wife, to inform her of his adventure, but was told she was not returned from market. He waited impatiently for her return, when he sprang up to meet her, crying, " Wife, I have done something to-day that will astonish you. I have performed a marvellous exploit!" "Patience!" says his wife. "Perhaps I have done something my-self to match it. But hear my story, and then talk of cleverness, if you please." The husband desired her to proceed.

"When I went to market," says she, "I found a man in want of thread. I showed him mine, which he approved of, and having bargained for it, he agreed to pay me accord-ing to the weight. I told him it weighed so much, which he seemed to discredit, and weighed it himself. Observing it to fall short of the weight I had mentioned, and fearing I should lose the price I at first expected, I requested him to weigh it over again, and make certain. In the meantime, taking an opportunity unobserved, I stripped off my silver bracelets and put them slily into the scale with my thread. The scale, of course, now preponderated, and I received the full price I had demanded." Having finished her story, she cried out, "Now, what do you think of your wife?" "Amazing! amazing!' said he. "Your capacity is supernatural. And now, if you please, I will give you a specimen of mine," and he related his adventure at the market. "O husband," she exclaimed when he had told his story, "had we not possessed such consummate wisdom and address, how could we have contrived means to repair our old house? In future vex not yourself about domestic concerns, since by the exercise of our talents we need never want for anything!"

The exploits of that precious pair may be compared with the following: An alewife went to the market with a brood of chickens and an old black hen. For the hen and one chicken she could not find a purchaser; so, before leaving the town, she called upon a surgeon, to try to effect a sale. He bought the chicken, but declined taking the hen. She then asked him if he would draw a tooth for it. The tooth was drawn, and he expressed his surprise on finding it was perfectly sound. "Oh," said she, "I knew it was sound; but it was worth while having it drawn for the old hen." She then called upon another surgeon, and had a second tooth drawn, as sound as the other. "What's to pay?" she inquired. "A shilling," said the surgeon. "Very well," rejoined the hostess, with a chuckle; "you left a shilling due in my house the other night, and now we are quits." "Certainly we are," responded the perplexed tooth-drawer, and the delighted old woman returned to her hostelry, to acquaint all her gossips of how cleverly she had outwitted the doctors.

Ferrier says, in his *Illustrations of Sterne*, that the facetious tales of the Sieur Gaulard laid the foundation of some of the jests in our old English collections. A few of them found their way somehow into Taylor's *Wit and Mirth*, and this is one : A monsieur chanced to meet a lady of his acquaintance, and asked her how she did and how her good husband fared, at which she wept, saying that her husband was in heaven. "In heaven!" quoth he. "It is the first time that I heard of it, and I am sorry for it with all my heart."

Similar in its point is a story in *Archie Armstrong's Banquet of Jests :*[1] Sitting over a cup of ale in a winter night, two widows entered into discourse of their dead husbands, and after ripping up their good and bad qualities, saith one of them to the maid, "I prithee, wench, reach us another light, for my

[1] Archie Armstrong was Court jester to James I. of England. It is needless, perhaps, to say that he had no hand in this book of facetiæ, which is composed for the most part of jests taken out of earlier collections.

husband (God rest his soul!) above all things loved to see good lights about the house. God grant him light everlasting!" "And I pray you, neighbour," said the other, "let the maid lay on some more coals or stir up the fire, for my husband in his lifetime ever loved to see a good fire. God grant him fire everlasting!"

This seems cousin-german to the Arabian story of two men, one of whom hailed from the town of Hama (ancient Hamath), the other from Hums (ancient Emessa). Those towns are not far apart, but the people of the former have the reputation of being very clever, while those of the latter are proverbially as stupid. (And for the proper understanding of the jest it should perhaps be explained that the Arabic verb *hama* means to "protect" or "defend," the verb *hamasa* to "roast" or "toast.") These men had some business of importance with the nearest magistrate, and set out together on their journey. The man of Hums, conscious of his own ignorance, begged his companion to speak first in the audience, in order that he might get a hint as to how such a formal matter should be conducted. Accordingly, when they came into the pasha's presence, the man of Hama went forward, and the pasha asked him, "Where are you from?"

" Your servant is from Hama," said he. " May Allah PROTECT (*hama*) your excellency!" The pasha then turned to the other man, and asked, "And where are you from?" to which he answered, "Your servant is from Hums. May Allah ROAST (*hamasa*) your excellency !"

Not a few of the *Bigarrures* of the Sieur Gaulard are the prototypes of bulls and foolish sayings of the typical Irishman, which go their ceaseless round in popular periodicals, and are even audaciously reproduced as original in our "comic" journals—save the mark! To cite some examples:

A friend one day told M. Gaulard that the Dean of Besançon was dead. "Believe it not," said he; "for had it been so he would have told me himself, since he writes to me about everything."

M. Gaulard asked his secretary one evening what hour it was. "Sir," replied the secretary, "I cannot tell you by the dial, because the sun is set." "Well," quoth M. Gaulard, "and can you not see by the candle?"

On another occasion the Sieur called from his bed to a servant desiring him to see if it was daylight yet. "There is no sign of daylight," said the servant. "I do not wonder," rejoined the Sieur, "that thou canst not see day, great fool as thou art. Take a candle and look with it out at the window, and thou shalt see whether it be day or not."

In a strange house, the Sieur found the walls of his bedchamber full of great holes. "This," exclaimed he in a rage, "is the cursedest chamber in all the world. One may see day all the night through."

Travelling in the country, his man, to gain the fairest way, rode through a field sowed with pease, upon which M. Gaulard cried to him, "Thou knave, wilt thou burn my horse's feet? Dost thou not know that about six weeks ago I burned my mouth with eating pease, they were so hot?"

A poor man complained to him that he had had a horse stolen from him. "Why did you not mark his visage," asked M. Gaulard, "and the clothes he wore?" "Sir," said the man, "I was not there when he was stolen." Quoth the Sieur, "You should have left somebody to ask him his name, and in what place he resided."

M. Gaulard felt the sun so hot in the midst of a field at noontide in August that he asked of those about him, "What means the sun to be so hot? How should it not keep its heat till winter, when it is cold weather?"

A proctor, discoursing with M. Gaulard, told him that a dumb, deaf, or blind man could not make a will but with certain additional forms. "I pray you," said the Sieur, "give me that in writing, that I may send it to a cousin of mine who is lame."

One day a friend visited the Sieur and found him asleep in his chair. "I slept," said he, "only to avoid idleness; for I must always be doing something."

The Abbé of Poupet complained to him that the moles had spoiled a fine meadow, and he could find no remedy for them. "Why, cousin," said M. Gaulard, "it is but paving your meadow, and the moles will no more trouble you."

M. Gaulard had a lackey belonging to Auvergne, who robbed him of twelve crowns and ran away, at which he was very angry, and said he would have nothing that came from that country. So he ordered all that was from Auvergne to be cast out of the house, even his mule; and to make the animal more ashamed, he caused his servants to take off its shoes and its saddle and bridle.

Although Taylor's *Wit and Mirth* is the most "original" of our old English jest-books

—that is to say, it contains very few stories in common with preceding collections—yet some of the diverting tales he relates are traceable to very distant sources, more especially the following :

A country fellow (that had not walked much in streets that were paved) came to London, where a dog came suddenly out of a house, and furiously ran at him. The fellow stooped to pick up a stone to cast at the dog, and finding them all fast rammed or paved in the ground, quoth he, "What a strange country am I in, where the people tie up the stones and let the dogs loose!"

Three centuries and a half before the Water Poet heard this exquisitely humorous story, the great Persian poet Sa'dí related it in his *Gulistán* (or Rose-garden), which was written A.D. 1278 :

A poor poet presented himself before the chief of a gang of robbers, and recited some verses in his praise. The robber-chief, however, instead of rewarding him, as he fondly expected, ordered him to be stripped of his clothes and expelled from the village. The dogs attacking him in the rear, the unlucky bard stooped to pick up a stone to throw at them, and finding the stones frozen in the ground, he exclaimed, "What a vile set of men are these, who set loose the dogs and fasten the stones ! "

Now here we have a very curious instance of the migration of a popular tale from Persia —perchance it first set out on its travels from India—in the thirteenth century, when grave and reverend seigniors wagged their beards and shook their portly sides at its recital, to London in the days of the Scottish Solomon (more properly dubbed "the wisest fool in Christendom"!), when Taylor, the Water Poet, probably heard it told, in some river-side tavern, amidst the clinking of beer-cans and the fragrant clouds blown from pipes of Trinidado, and "put it in his book!" How it came into England it would be interesting to ascertain. It may have been brought to Europe by the Venetian merchants, who traded largely in the Levant and with the Moors in Northern Africa.

CHAPTER IV

GOTHAMITE DROLLERIES (*continued*).

ALES of sharpers' tricks upon simpletons do not quite fall within the scope of the present series of papers, but there is one, in the *Arabian Nights*—not found, however, in our common English version of that fascinating story-book—which deserves a place among noodle-stories, since it is so diverting, is not very generally known, and is probably the original of the early Italian novel of the *Monk Transformed*, which is ascribed to Michele Colombo:

A rustic simpleton was walking homeward dragging his ass after him by the halter, which a brace of sharpers observing, one said to his fellow, "Come with me, and I will take the ass from that man." He then quietly advanced to the ass, unloosed it from the halter, and gave the animal to his companion, who went off with it, after which he put the halter over his own head, and allowed

6

the rustic to drag him for some little distance,
until he with the ass was fairly out of sight,
when he suddenly stopped, and the man
having tugged at the halter several times
without effect, looked round, and, amazed to
see a human being in place of his beast,
exclaimed, " Who art thou ? "   The sharper
answered, " I was thy ass ; but hear my story,
for it is wonderful.   I had a good and pious
mother, and one day I came home intoxicated.
Grieved to see me in such a state, she gently
reproved me, but I, instead of being pene-
trated with remorse, beat her with a stick,
whereupon she prayed to Allah, and, in
answer to her supplication, lo ! I was transformed into an ass.   In that shape I have
continued until this day, when my mother, as
it appears, has interceded for my restoration
to human form, as before."   The simpleton,
believing every word of this strange story,
raised his eyes to heaven, saying, " Of a truth
there is no power but from Allah !   But, pray,
forgive me for having used thee as I have
done."   The sharper readily granted his
forgiveness, and went off to rejoin his companion and dispose of the ass ; while the
simpleton returned home, and showing his
wife the bridle, told her of the marvellous
transformation which had occurred.   His
wife, in hopes of propitiating Heaven, gave

alms and offered up many prayers to avert
evil from them, on account of their having
used a human being as an ass. At length
the simpleton, having remained idle at home
for some time, went one day to the market to
purchase another ass, and on entering the place
where all the animals were fastened, he saw
with astonishment his old ass offered for sale.
Putting his mouth to its ear, he whispered,
"Woe to thee, unlucky!   Doubtless thou
hast again been intoxicated ; but, by Allah, I
will never buy thee ! "

Another noodle-story, of a different class,
in the *Arabian Nights*, may be here cited in
full from Sir R. F. Burton's translation of
that delightful work, privately printed for the
subscribers, and it will serve, moreover, as
a fair specimen of the admirable manner
in which that ripe scholar has represented in
English the quaint style of his original :
[Quoth one of the learned,] I passed once
by a school wherein a schoolmaster was
teaching children ; so I entered, finding him
a good-looking man, and a well-dressed,
when he rose to me and made me sit with
him. Then I examined him in the Korán,
and in syntax and prosody, and lexicography ;
and behold, he was perfect in all required of
him ; and I said to him, "Allah strengthen

thy purpose ! Thou art indeed versed in all
that is requisite." Thereafter I frequented
him a while, discovering daily some new
excellence in him, and quoth I to myself,
" This is indeed a wonder in any dominie ;
for the wise are agreed upon a lack of wit
in children's teachers." [1]   Then I separated
myself from him, and sought him and visited
him only every few days, till coming to see
him one day, as of wont, I found the school
shut, and made inquiry of his neighbours, who
replied, " Some one is dead in his house." So
I said in my mind, " It behoveth me to pay
him a visit of condolence," and going to his
house, knocked at the door, when a slave-girl
came out to me and asked, " What dost thou
want ? " and I answered, " I want thy master."
She replied, " He is sitting alone mourning ; "
and I rejoined, " Tell him that his friend
So-and-so seeketh to console him." She went
in and told him ; and he said, " Admit him."
So she brought me in to him, and I found
him seated alone, and his head bound with

[1] This notion, that schoolmasters "lack wit,"
however absurd, seems to have been entertained
from ancient times, and to be still prevalent in
the East ; the so-called jests of Hierokles are all
at the expense of pedants ; and the Turkish
typical noodle is Khoja (*i.e.*, Teacher) Nasru-'d-
Dín, some of whose " witless devices " shall be
cited presently.

mourning fillets. So I said to him, "Allah
requite thee amply! This is a path all must
perforce tread, and it behoveth thee to take
patience," adding, "but who is dead unto
thee?" He answered, "One who was dearest
of the folk to me, and best beloved." "Perhaps
thy father?" "No." "Thy brother?" "No."
"One of thy kindred?" "No." Then asked
I, "What relation was the dead to thee?"
and he answered, "My lover." Quoth I to
myself, "This is the first proof to swear by
of his lack of wit." So I said to him, "Assuredly there be others than she, and fairer;"
and he made answer, "I never saw her that
I might judge whether or no there be others
fairer than she." Quoth I to myself, "This
is another proof positive." Then I said to
him, "And how couldst thou fall in love with
one thou hast never seen?" He replied,
"Know that I was sitting one day at the
window, when, lo! there passed by a man,
singing the following distich:

> "'Umm Amr', thy boons Allah repay!
> Give back my heart, be't where it may!'"

The schoolmaster continued, "When I heard
the man humming these words as he passed
along the street, I said to myself, 'Except this
Umm Amrú were without equal in the world,
the poets had not celebrated her in ode and

canzon.' So I fell in love with her; but two days after, the same man passed, singing the following couplet :

> " ' Ass and Umm Amr' went their way,
>   Nor she nor ass returned for aye.'

Thereupon I knew that she was dead, and mourned for her. This was three days ago, and I have been mourning ever since." So I left him and fared forth, having assured myself of the weakness of the gerund-grinder's wit. [1]

Here, surely, was the very Father of Folly, but what shall we say of judges and magistrates being sometimes (represented as) equally witless? Thus we are told, among the cases decided by a Turkish Kází, that two men came before him one of whom complained that the other had almost bit his ear off. The accused denied this, and declared that the fellow had bit his own ear. After pondering the matter for some time, the judge told them to come again two hours later. Then he went into his private room,

[1] *Elf Layla wa Layla,* or, The Book of a Thousand Nights and a Night. Translated, with Introduction, Notes on the Manners and Customs of Moslem Men, and a Terminal Essay on the History of *The Nights,* by R. F. Burton.   Vol. v.

and attempted to bring his ear and his mouth together ; but all he did was to fall backwards and break his head. Wrapping a cloth round his head, he returned to court, and the two men coming in again presently, he thus decided the question : "No man can bite his own ear, but in trying to do so he may fall down and break his head."

A Sinhalese story, which is also well known in various forms in India, furnishes a still more remarkable example of forensic sagacity. It is thus related by the able editor of *The Orientalist*, vol. i., p. 191 :

One night some thieves broke into the house of a rich man, and carried away all his valuables. The man complained to the justice of the peace, who had the robbers captured, and when brought before him, inquired of them whether they had anything to say in their defence. "Sir," said they, "we are not to blame in this matter; the robbery was entirely due to the mason who built the house ; for the walls were so badly made, and gave way so easily, that we were quite unable to resist the temptation of breaking in." Orders were then given to bring the mason to the court-house. On his arrival he was informed of the charge brought against him. "Ah," said he, "the fault is not mine, but that of the coolie, who made mortar

badly." When the coolie was brought, he laid
the blame on the potter, who, he said, had
sold him a cracked chattie, in which he could
not carry sufficient water to mix the mortar
properly. Then the potter was brought before
the judge, and he explained that the blame
should not be laid upon him, but upon a very
pretty woman, who, in a beautiful dress, was
passing at the time he was making the chattie,
and had so riveted his attention, that he forgot
all about the work. When the woman appeared, she protested that the fault was not
hers, for she would not have been in that
neighbourhood at all had the goldsmith sent
home her earrings at the proper time; the
charge, she argued, should properly be brought
against him. The goldsmith was brought, and
as he was unable to offer any reasonable
excuse, he was condemned to be hanged.
Those in the court, however, begged the
judge to spare the goldsmith's life; "for,"
said they, "he is very sick and ill-favoured,
and would not make at all a pretty spectacle."
"But," said the judge, "somebody must be
hanged." Then they drew the attention of
the court to the fact that there was a fat
Moorman in a shop opposite, who was a much
fitter subject for an execution, and asked that
he might be hanged in the goldsmith's stead.
The learned judge, considering that this

arrangement would be very satisfactory, gave judgment accordingly.

If some of the last-cited stories are not precisely Gothamite drolleries, though all are droll enough in their way, there can be no doubt whatever that we have a Sinhalese brother to the men of Gotham in the following: A villager in Ceylon, whose calf had got its head into a pot and could not get it out again, sent for a friend, celebrated for his wisdom, to release the poor animal. The sagacious friend, taking in the situation at a glance, cut off the calf's head, broke the pot, and then delivered the head to the owner of the calf, saying, "What will you do when I am dead and gone?"—And we have another Gothamite in the Kashmírí who bought as much rice as he thought would suffice for a year's food, and finding he had only enough for eleven months, concluded it was better to fast the other month right off, which he did accordingly; but he died just before the month was completed, leaving eleven months' rice in his house.

The typical noodle of the Turks, the Khoja Nasru-'d-Dín, is said to have been a subject of the independent prince of Karaman, at whose capital, Konya, he resided, and he is represented as a contemporary of Tímúr (Tamerlane), in the middle of the fourteenth century. The pleasantries which are ascribed to him are for the most part common to all countries, but some are probably of genuine Turkish origin. To cite a few specimens: The Khoja's wife said to him one day, "Make me a present of a kerchief of red Yemen silk, to put on my head." The Khoja stretched out his arms and said, "Like that? Is that large enough?" On her replying in the affirmative he ran off to the bazaar, with his arms still stretched out, and meeting a man on the road, he bawled to him, "Look where you are going, O man, or you will cause me to lose my measure!"

Another day the Khoja's wife washed his caftan and spread it upon a tree in the garden of the house. That night the Khoja goes out, and thinks he sees in the moonlight a man motionless upon a tree in the garden. "Give me my bow and arrows," said he to his wife, and having received them, he shot the caftan, piercing it through and through, and then returned into the house. Next morning, when he discovered that it was his own caftan he had shot at, he exclaimed, "By Allah, had I happened to be in it, I should have killed myself!"

The Ettrick Shepherd's well-known story of the two Highlanders and the wild boar has its exact parallel in the Turkish jest-book, as follows: One day the Khoja went with his friend Sheragh Ahmed to the den ot a wolf, in order to take the cubs. Said the Khoja to Ahmed, "Do you go in, and I will watch without;" and Ahmed went in, to take the cubs in the absence of the old wolf. But she came back presently, and had got half-way into her den when the Khoja seized hold of her tail. The wolf in her struggles cast up a great dust into the eyes of Ahmed, who called out to the Khoja, "Hallo! what does all this dust mean?" The Khoja replied, "If the wolf's tail breaks, you will soon know what the dust means!"

Several of the jests closely resemble "Joe Millers" told of Irishmen, such as this: It happened one night, after the Khoja and a guest had lain down to sleep, that the taper went out. "O Khoja Effendi," said the guest, "the taper is gone out. But there is a taper at your right side. Pray bring it and let us light it." Quoth the Khoja, "You must surely be a fool to think that I should know my right hand in the dark." And this: A thief having stolen a piece of salted cheese from the Khoja, he ran immediately and seated himself on the border of a fountain. Said the people to him,

"O Khoja, what have you come here to look for in such a hurry?" The Khoja replied, "The thief will certainly come here to drink as soon as he has eaten my salted cheese; I always do so myself."

And here is one of the Gothamite class: One evening the Khoja went to the well to draw water, and seeing the moon reflected in the water, he exclaimed, "The moon has fallen into the well; I must pull it out." So he let down the rope and hook, and the hook became fastened to a stone, whereupon he exerted all his strength, and the rope broke, and he fell upon his back. Looking into the sky, he saw the moon, and cried out joyfully, "Praise be to Allah! I am sorely bruised, but the moon has got into its place again."

There is a well-worn jest of an Irishman who, being observed by a friend to look exceedingly blank and perplexed, was asked what ailed him. He replied that he had had a dream. "Was it a good or a bad dream?" "Faith," said he, "it was a little of both; but I'll tell ye. I dreamt that I was with the Pope, who was the finest gentleman in the whole district; and after we had conversed a while, his Holiness axed me, Would I drink? Thinks I to myself, 'Would a duck swim?' So, seeing the whisky and the lemons and the sugar on the side-board, I said, I didn't mind if I took a drop of punch. 'Cold or hot?' says his Holiness. 'Hot, your Holiness,' says I. So on that he steps down to the kitchen for the boiling water, but, bedad, before he came back, I woke straight up; and now it's distressing me that I didn't take it cold!"

We have somewhat of a parallel to this in a Turkish jest: The Khoja dreamt that some one gave him nine pieces of money, but he was not content, and said, "Make it ten." Then he awoke and found his hands empty. Instantly closing his eyes again, and holding out his hand, he said, "I repent; give me the nine pieces."[1]

But the Chinese relate the very counterpart of our Irishman's story. A confirmed drunkard dreamt that he had been presented with a cup of excellent wine, and set it by the fire to warm,[2] that he should better enjoy the flavour of it; but just as he was about to drink off the delicious draught he awoke.

[1] The Khoja, however, was not such a fool as we might conclude from the foregoing examples of his sayings and doings; for, being asked one day what musical instrument he liked best, he answered, "I am very fond of the music of plates and saucepans."

[2] In China wine is almost invariably taken hot. Irishmen generally drink their whisky "nate."

"Fool that I am," he cried, "why was I not content to drink it cold?"[1]

———————

The Chinese seem to have as keen a sense of humour as any other people. They tell a story, for instance, of a lady who had been recently married, and on the third day saw her husband returning home, so she slipped quietly behind him and gave him a hearty kiss. The husband was annoyed, and said she offended all propriety. "Pardon! pardon!" said she. "I did not know it was you." Thus the excuse may sometimes be worse than the offence. There is exquisite humour in the following noodle-story: Two brothers were tilling the ground together. The elder, having prepared dinner, called his brother, who replied in a loud voice, "Wait till I have hidden my spade, and I shall at once be with you." When he joined his elder brother, the latter mildly reproached him, saying, "When one hides anything, one should keep silence, or at least should not cry aloud about it, for it lays one open to be robbed." Dinner over,

[1] This and the following specimens of Chinese stories of simpletons are from "Contes et Bon Mots extraits d'un livre chinois intitulé *Siao li Siao*, traduit par M. Stanislas Julien," (*Journal Asiatique*, tom. iv., 1824).

the younger went back to the field, and looked
for his spade, but could not find it ; so he
ran to his brother and *whispered* mysteriously
in his ear, " My spade is stolen! "—The
passion for collecting antique relics is thus
ridiculed : A man who was fond of old
curiosities, though he knew not the true from
the false, expended all his wealth in purchas-
ing mere imitations of the lightning-stick of
Tchew-Koung, a glazed cup of the time of the
Emperor Cheun, and the mat of Confucius ;
and being reduced to beggary, he carried
these spurious relics about with him, and said
to the people in the streets, " Sirs, I pray you,
give me some coins struck by Taï-Koung."

Indian fiction abounds in stories of simpletons, and probably the oldest extant drolleries
of the Gothamite type are found in the
Jâtakas, or Buddhist Birth-stories. Assuredly
they were own brothers to our mad men of
Gotham, the Indian villagers who, being
pestered by mosquitoes when at work in the
forest, bravely resolved, according to *Jâtaka*
44, to take their bows and arrows and other
weapons and make war upon the troublesome
insects until they had shot dead or cut in
pieces every one ; but in trying to shoot the
mosquitoes they only shot, struck, and injured

one another. And nothing more foolish is recorded of the Schildburgers than Somadeva relates, in his *Kathá Sarit Ságara*, of the simpletons who cut down the palm-trees: Being required to furnish the king with a certain quantity of dates, and perceiving that it was very easy to gather the dates of a palm which had fallen down of itself, they set to work and cut down all the date-palms in their village, and having gathered from them their whole crop of dates, they raised them up and planted them again, thinking they would grow.

In illustration of the apothegm that "fools who attend only to the words of an order, and do not understand the meaning, cause much detriment," is the story of the servants who kept the rain off the trunks: The camel of a merchant gave way under its load on a journey. He said to his servants, "I will go and buy another camel to carry the half of this camel's load. And you must remain here, and take particular care that if it clouds over the rain does not wet the leather of these trunks, which are full of clothes." With these words the merchant left the servants by the side of the camel and went off, and suddenly a cloud came up and began to discharge rain. Then the fools said, "Our master told us to take care that the rain did not touch the leather of the trunks;" and after they had made this sage reflection they dragged the clothes out of the trunks and wrapped them round the leather. The consequence was that the rain spoiled the clothes. Then the merchant returned, and in a rage said to his servants, "You rascals! Talk of water! Why, the whole stock of clothes is spoiled by the rain!" And they answered him, "You told us to keep the rain off the leather of the trunks. What fault have we committed?" He answered, "I told you that if the leather got wet the clothes would be spoiled. I told you so in order to save the clothes, not the leather."

The story of the servant who looked after the door is a farther illustration of the same maxim. A merchant said to his foolish servant, "Take care of the door of my shop; I am going home for a short time." After his master was gone, the fool took the shop-door on his shoulder and went off to see an actor perform. As he was returning his master met him, and gave him a scolding, and he answered, "I have taken care of this door, as you told me."

This jest had found its way into Europe three centuries ago. It is related of Giufa, the typical Sicilian booby, and probably came to England from Italy. This is how it is told in the *Sacke Full of Newes*, a jest-book

originally printed in the sixteenth century:
"In the countrey dwelt a Gentlewoman who
had a French man dwelling with her, and he
did ever use to go to Church with her; and
upon a time he and his mistresse were going
to church, and she bad him pull the doore
after him and follow her to the church; and
so he took the doore betweene his armes, and
lifted it from the hooks, and followed his
mistresse with it.   But when she looked
behinde her and saw him bring the doore
upon his back, 'Why, thou foolish knave,'
qd she, 'what wilt thou do with the door?'
'Marry, mistresse,' qd he, 'you bad me pull
the doore after me.'   'Why, fool,' qd she, 'I
did command thee that thou shouldest make
fast the doore after thee, and not bring it upon
thy back after me.'   But after this there was
much good sport and laughing at his simplicity and foolishnesse therein."

In the capacity of a merchant the simpleton
does very wonderful things, and plumes himself on his sagacity, as we have already seen
in the case of the Arab and his cow.   And
here are a brace of similar stories: A foolish
man once went to the island of Katáha to
trade, and among his wares was a quantity of
fragrant aloes-wood.   After he had sold his
other goods, he could not find any one to take
the aloes-wood off his hands, for the people

who live there are not acquainted with that article of commerce. Then seeing people buying charcoal from the woodmen, he burnt his stock of aloes-wood and reduced it to charcoal. He sold it for the price which charcoal usually fetched, and returning home, boasted of his cleverness, and became the laughing-stock of everybody.—Another block-head went to the market to sell cotton, but no one would buy it from him, because it was not properly cleaned. In the meanwhile he saw in the bazaar a goldsmith selling gold which he had purified by heating it, and he saw it taken by a customer. Seeing that, he threw his cotton into the fire in order to purify it, and it was all burned to ashes.

There must be few who have not heard of the Irishman who was hired by a Yarmouth maltster to help in loading a ship. As the vessel was about to sail, the Irishman cried out from the quay, "Captain, I lost your shovel overboard, but I cut a big notch on the rail-fence, round the stern, just where it went down, so you will find it when you come back."—A similar story is told of an Indian simpleton. He was sailing in a ship when he let a silver cup fall from his hand into the water. Having taken notes of the spot by observing the eddies and other signs in the water, he said to himself, " I will bring it up from the bottom when I return." As he was recrossing the sea, he saw the eddies and other signs, and thinking he recognised the spot, he plunged into the water again and again, to recover his cup, but he only got well laughed at for his pains.

We have an amusing commentary on the maxim that " distress is sure to come from being in the company of fools " in the following, from the Canarese story-book entitled *Kathá Manjari:* A foolish fellow travelled with a shopkeeper. When it became dark, the fool lay down in the road to sleep, but the shopkeeper took shelter in a hollow tree. Presently some thieves came along the road, and one struck his feet against the fool's legs, upon which he exclaimed to his companions, " What is this ? Is it a piece of wood ?" The fool was angry, and said, " Go away ! go away ! Is there a knot, well tied, containing five annas, in the loins of a plank in your house ?" The thieves then seized him, and took away his annas. As they were moving off, they asked if the money was good or bad, to which the noodle replied, " Ha ! ha ! is it of my money you speak in that way, and want to know whether it is good or bad ? Look—there is a shopkeeper in that tree," pointing with his finger—" show it to him." Then the thieves went up to the shopkeeper and robbed him of two hundred pagodas.

In our next story, of the villagers who ate the buffalo, is exemplified the fact that " fools, in the conceit of their folly, while they deny what need not be denied, reveal what it is their interest to suppress, in order to get themselves believed." Some villagers took a buffalo belonging to a certain man, and killed it in an enclosure outside the village, under a banyan tree, and dividing the flesh, ate it up. The owner of the buffalo went and complained to the king, and he had the villagers who had eaten the animal brought before him. The proprietor of the buffalo said before the king, in their presence, " These men took my buffalo under a banyan tree near the tank, and killed and ate it before my eyes," whereupon an old fool among the villagers said, " There is no tank or banyan tree in our village. He says what is not true ; where did we kill his buffalo or eat it ? " When the man heard this, he replied, "What ! are there not a banyan tree and a tank on the east side of the village ? Moreover, you ate my buffalo on the eighth day of the lunar month." The old fool then said, " There is no east side or eighth day in our village." On hearing this, the king laughed, and said, to encourage the fool, "You are a truthful person ; you never say anything false ;

so tell me the truth: did you eat that buffalo, or did you not ?" The old fool answered, " I was born three years after my father died, and he taught me skill in speaking. So I never say what is untrue, my king. It is true that we ate his buffalo, but all the rest that he alleges is false." When the king heard this, he and his courtiers could not restrain their laughter; but he restored the price of the buffalo to the man, and fined the villagers.

But sometimes even kings have been arrant noodles, and their credulity quite as amusing —or amazing—as that of their subjects. Once on a time there was a king who had a handsome daughter, and he summoned his physicians, and said to them, " Make some preparation of salutary drugs, which will cause my daughter to grow up quickly, so that she may be married to a good husband." The physicians, wishing to get a living out of this royal fool, replied, " There is a medicine which will do this, but it can only be procured in a distant country; and while we are sending for it, we must shut up your daughter in concealment, for this is the treatment laid down in such cases." The king having consented, they placed his daughter in concealment for several years, pretending that they were engaged in procuring the medicine; and when she was grown up, they presented her to the king, saying that she had been made to grow by the preparation ; so the king was highly pleased, and gave them much wealth.

Between an Indian rájá and an Indian dhobie, or washerman, there is the greatest possible difference socially, but individually —when both are noodles—there may be sometimes very little to choose; indeed, of the two, all things considered, the difference, if any, is perhaps in favour of the humble cleanser of body-clothes. A favourite story in various parts of India, near akin to that last cited, is of a poor washerman and his young ass. This simpleton one day, passing a school kept by a mullah, or Muhammedan doctor of laws, heard him scolding his pupils, exclaiming that they were still asses, although he had done so much to make them men. The washerman thought that here was a rare chance, for he happened to have the foal of the ass that carried his bundles of clothes, which, since he had no child, he should get the learned mullah to change into a boy. Thus thinking, he goes next day to the mullah, and asks him to admit his foal into his school, in order that it should be changed into the human form and nature. The preceptor, seeing the poor fellow's simplicity, answered that the task was very laborious, and he must have a fee of a hundred rupís. So the washerman went home, and soon returned leading his foal, which, with the money, he handed over to the teacher, who told him to come again on such a day and hour, when he should find that the change he desired had been effected. But the washer-man was so impatient that he went to the teacher several times before the day appointed, and was informed that the foal was beginning to learn manners, that its ears were already become very much shorter, and, in short, that it was making satisfactory progress.

It happened, when the day came on which he was to receive his young ass transformed into a fine, well-educated boy, the simpleton was kept busy with his customers' clothes, but on the day following he found time to go to the teacher, who told him it was most un-fortunate he had not come at the appointed hour, since the youth had quitted the school yesterday, refusing to submit any longer to authority; but the teacher had just learned that he had been made kází (or judge) in Cawnpore. At first the washerman was disposed to be angry, but reflecting that, after all, the business was better even than he anticipated, he thanked the preceptor for all his care and trouble, and returned home.

Having informed his wife of his good luck, they resolved to visit their quondam young foal, and get him to make them some allowance out of his now ample means. So, shutting up their house, they travelled to Cawnpore, which they reached in safety. Being directed to the kází's court, the washerman, leaving his wife outside, entered, and discovered the kází seated in great dignity, and before him were the pleaders, litigants, and officers of the court. He had brought a bridle in one hand and a wisp of hay in the other; but being unable, on account of the crowd, to approach the kází, he got tired of waiting, so, holding up the bridle and the hay, he cried out, "Khoor! khoor! khoor!" as he used to do in calling his donkeys, thinking this would induce the kází to come to him. But, instead of this, he was seized by the kází's order and locked up for creating a disturbance.

When the business of the court was over, the kází, pitying the supposed madman, sent for him to learn the reason of his strange behaviour, and in answer to his inquiries the simpleton said, "You don't seem to know me, sir, nor recognise this bridle, which has been in your mouth so often. You appear to forget that you are the foal of one of my asses, that I got changed into a man, for the fee of a hundred rupís, by a learned mullah who transforms asses into educated men. You forget what you were, and, I suppose, will be as little submissive to me as you were to the mullah when you ran away from him." All present were convulsed with laughter: such a "case" was never heard of before. But the kází, seeing how the mullah had taken advantage of the poor fellow's simplicity, gave him a present of a hundred rupís, besides sufficient for the expenses of his journey home, and so dismissed him.

A party of rogues once found as great a blockhead in a rich Indian herdsman, to whom they said, "We have asked the daughter of a wealthy inhabitant of the town in marriage for you, and her father has promised to give her." He was much pleased to hear this, and gave them an ample reward for their trouble. After a few days they came again and told him that his marriage had taken place. Again he gave them rich presents for their good news. Some more days having passed, they said to him, "A son has been born to you," at which he was in ecstacies and gave them all his remaining wealth; but the next day, when he began to lament, saying, " I am longing to see my son," the people laughed at him on account of his

having been cheated by the rogues, as if he
had acquired the stupidity of cattle from
having so much to do with them.

It is not generally known that the incident
which forms the subject of the droll Scotch
song "The Barring of the Door," which also
occurs in the *Nights* of Straparola, is of
Eastern origin. In an Arabian tale, a blockhead, having married his pretty cousin, gave
the customary feast to their relations and
friends. When the festivities were over, he
conducted his guests to the door, and from
absence of mind neglected to shut it before
returning to his wife. "Dear cousin," said
his wife to him when they were alone, "go
and shut the street door." "It would be
strange indeed," he replied, "if I did such a
thing. Am I just made a bridegroom, clothed
in silk, wearing a shawl and a dagger set with
diamonds, and am I to go and shut the door?
Why, my dear, you are crazy. Go and shut
it yourself." "Oh, indeed!" exclaimed the
wife. "Am I, young, robed in a dress, with
lace and precious stones—am I to go and
shut the street door? No, indeed! It is you
who are become crazy, and not I. Come, let
us make a bargain," she continued; "and
let the first who speaks go and fasten the
door." "Agreed," said the husband, and immediately he became mute, and the wife too

was silent, while they both sat down, dressed as they were in their nuptial attire, looking at each other and seated on opposite sofas. Thus they remained for two hours. Some thieves happened to pass by, and seeing the door open, entered and laid hold of whatever came to their hands. The silent couple heard footsteps in the house, but opened not their mouths. The thieves came into the room and saw them seated motionless and apparently indifferent to all that might take place. They continued their pillage, therefore, collecting together everything valuable, and even dragging away the carpets from beneath them; they laid hands on the noodle and his wife, taking from their persons every article of jewellery, while they, in fear of losing the wager, said not a word. Having thus cleared the house, the thieves departed quietly, but the pair continued to sit, uttering not a syllable. Towards morning a police officer came past on his tour of inspection, and seeing the door open, walked in. After searching all the rooms and finding no person, he entered their apartment, and inquired the meaning of what he saw. Neither of them would condescend to reply. The officer became angry, and ordered their heads to be cut off. The executioner's sword was about to perform its office, when the wife cried out,

"Sir, he is my husband. Do not kill him!"
"Oh, oh," exclaimed the husband, overjoyed
and clapping his hands, "you have lost the
wager; go and shut the door." He then explained the whole affair to the police officer,
who shrugged his shoulders and went away.[1]

A party of noodles are substituted for the
husband and wife in a Turkish version
of the tale, in the *History of the Forty Vazírs.*
Some bang-eaters,[2] while out walking,
found a sequin. They said, "Let us go
to a cook, and buy food and eat." So they
went and entered a cook's shop and said,
"Master, give us a sequin's worth of food."
The cook prepared all kinds of food, and
loaded a porter with it; and the bang-eaters

---

[1] In another Arabian version, the man desires
his wife to moisten some stale bread she has set
before him for supper, and she refuses. After an
altercation it is agreed that the one who speaks
first shall get up and moisten the bread. A
neighbour comes in, and, to his surprise, finds the
couple dumb; he kisses the wife, but the man
says nothing; he gives the man a blow, but still
he says nothing; he has the man taken before
the kází, but even yet he says nothing; the kází
orders him to be hanged, and he is led off to
execution, when the wife rushes up and cries
out, "Oh, save my poor husband!" "You
wretch," says the man, "go home and moisten
the bread!"

[2] Bang is a preparation of hemp and coarse
opium.

took him without the city, where there was a
ruined tomb, which they entered and sat
down in, and the porter deposited the food
and went away. The bang-eaters began to
partake of the food, when suddenly one of
them said, "The door is open ; do one of you
shut it, else some other bang-eaters will come
in and annoy us : even though they be friends,
they will do the deeds of foes." One of them
replied, "Go thou and shut the door," and
they fell a-quarrelling. At length one said,
"Come, let us agree that whichever of us
speaks or laughs shall rise and fasten the
door." They all agreed to this proposal, and
left the food and sat quite still. Suddenly a
great number of dogs came in ; not one of the
bang-eaters stirred or spoke, for if one spoke
he would have to rise and shut the door, so
they spoke not. The dogs made an end of
the food, and ate it all up. Just then another
dog leapt in from without, but no food remained. Now one of the bang-eaters had
partaken of everything, and some of the food
remained about his mouth and on his beard.
That newly come dog licked up the particles
of food that were on the bang-eater's breast,
and while he was licking up those about his
mouth, he took his lip for a piece of meat
and bit it. The bang-eater did not stir, for
he said within himself, "They will tell me to

shut the door." But to ease his soul he cried,
" Ough !" inwardly cursing the dog. When
the other bang-eaters heard him make that
noise, they said, " Rise, fasten the door."
He replied, "After loss, attention ! Now that
the food is gone, and my lip is wounded,
what is the use of shutting that door ?" and
crying, " Woe l alas !" they each went in a
different direction.[1]

A similar story is known in Kashmír : Five
friends chanced to meet, and all having
leisure, they decided to go to the bazaar and
purchase a sheep's head, and have a great
feast in the house of one of the party, each
of whom subscribed four annas. The head
was bought, but while they were returning to
the house it was remembered that there was
not any butter. On this one of the five pro-
posed that the first of them that should break
silence by speaking should go for the butter.
Now it was no light matter to have to retrace
one's steps back to the butter-shop, as the
way was long and the day was very hot. So
they all five kept strict silence. Pots were
cleaned, the fire was prepared, and the head
laid thereon. Now and then one would
cough, and another would groan, but never a
tongue uttered a word, though the fire was

[1] From Mr. E. J. W. Gibb's translation of the
Forty Vazirs (London : 1886).

fast going out, and the head was getting burnt, owing to there being no fat or butter wherewith to grease the pot. Thus matters were when a policeman passed by, and, attracted by the smell of cooking, looked in at the window, and saw these five men perfectly silent and sitting around a burnt sheep's head. Not knowing the arrangement, he supposed that these men were either mad or were thieves, and so he inquired how they came there, and how they obtained the head. Not a word was uttered in reply. "Why are you squatting there in that stupid fashion?" shouted the policeman. Still no reply. Then the policeman, full of rage that these wretched men should thus mock at his authority, took them all off straight to the police inspector's office. On arrival the inspector asked them the reason of their strange behaviour, but he also got no reply. This rather tried the patience and temper of the man of authority, who was generally feared, and flattered, and bribed. So he ordered one of the five to be immediately flogged. The poor fool bore it bravely, and uttered never a sound ; but when the blows repeatedly fell on the same wounded parts, he could endure no longer, and cried out, "Oh! oh! Why do you beat me ? Enough, enough! Is it not enough that the sheep's head has been spoiled ?"

His four associates now cried out, "Go to the bazaar and fetch the butter."[1]

There is quite as droll a version current among the people of Ceylon, to the following effect : A gentleman once had in his employment twenty-five idiots. In the old times it was customary with Sinhalese high families not to allow their servants to eat from plates, but every day they were supplied with plantain leaves, from which they took their food. After eating, they were accustomed to shape the leaf into the form of a cup and drink out of it. Now in this gentleman's house the duty of providing the leaves devolved upon the twenty-five idiots, who were scarcely fit for any other work. One day, when they had gone into the garden to cut the leaves, they spoke among themselves and said, " Why should we, every one of us, trouble ourselves to fetch plantain leaves, when one only could very easily do it ? Let us therefore lie down on the ground and sleep

[1] Knowles' *Dictionary of Kashmiri Proverbs and Sayings*, pp. 197-8. The article bought by the five men is called a *hir*, which Mr. Knowles says " is the head of any animal used for food," and a *sheep's* head were surely fitting food for such noodles. Mr. Knowles makes it appear that the whole affair of keeping silence was a mere jest, but we have before seen that it is decidedly meant for a noodle-story.

like dead men, and let him who first utters a
sound or opens his eyes undertake the work."
It was no sooner said than done. The men
lay in a heap like so many logs. At break-
fast-time that day the hungry servants went
to the kitchen for their rice, only to be
disappointed.   No leaves were forthcoming
on which to distribute the food, and a complaint was made to the master that the
twenty-five idiots had not returned to the
house since they went out in the morning.
Search was at once made, and they were
found fast asleep in the garden. After vainly
endeavouring to rouse them, the master
concluded that they were dead, and ordered
his servants to dig a deep hole and bury
them. A grave was then dug, and the idiots
were, one by one, thrown into it, but still
there was no noise or motion on their part.
At length, when they were all put into the
grave, and were being covered up, a tool
employed by one of the servants hit sharply
by accident against the leg of one of the
idiots, who then involuntarily moaned. Thereupon all the others exclaimed, "You were
the first to utter a sound; therefore from
henceforth you must take upon yourself the
duty of providing the plantain leaves." [1]

It has already been remarked that a literary

[1] *The Orientalist,* 1884, p. 136.

Italian version of the Silent Couple is found
in the *Nights* of Straparola, but there are
other variants orally current among the com
mon people in different parts of Italy. This
is one from Venice : There were once a
husband and a wife. The former said one
day to the latter, " Let us have some fritters. "
She replied, " What shall we do for a frying-
pan ? " " Go and borrow one from my godmother." "You go ·and get it ; it is only
a little way off." " Go yourself, and I will
take it back when we are done with it." So
she went and borrowed the pan, and when
she returned said to her husband, " Here is
the pan, but you must carry it back." So
they cooked the fritters, and after they had
eaten, the husband said, " Now let us go to
work, both of us, and the one who speaks first
shall carry back the pan." Then she began
to spin, and he to draw his thread—for he
was a shoemaker—and all the time keeping
silence, except that when he drew his thread
he said, "Leulerò ! leulerò ! " and she, spinning, answered, " Picicì ! picicì ! picicìò ! "
And they said not another word. Now there
happened to pass that way a soldier with
a horse, and he asked a woman if there was
any shoemaker in that street. She said there
was one near by, and took him to the house.
The، soldier asked the shoemaker to come

and cut his horse a girth, and he would pay
him. The latter made no answer but " Leulerò! leulerò!" and his wife "Picicì! picicì!
piciciò!" Then the soldier said, "Come and
cut my horse a girth, or I will cut your head
óff." The shoemaker only answered, " Leulerò! leulerò!" and his wife "Picicì! picicì!
piciciò!" Then the soldier began to grow
angry, and seized his sword, and said to the
shoemaker, "Either come and cut my horse
a girth, or I will cut your head off." But to
no purpose. The shoemaker did not wish to
be the first one to speak, and only replied,
"Leulerò! leulerò!" and his wife "Picicì!
picicì! piciciò!" Then the soldier got mad in
good earnest, seized the shoemaker's head,
and was going to cut it off. When his wife
saw that, she cried out, "Ah, don't, for
mercy's sake!" "Good!" exclaimed her
husband, "good! Now you go and carry the
pan back to my godmother, and I will go and
cut the horse's girth."

In a Sicilian version the man and wife fry
some fish, and then set about their respective
work—shoemaking and spinning—and the
one who finishes first the piece of work begun
is to eat the fish. While they are singing
and whistling at their work, a friend comes
along, who knocks at the door, but receives
no answer. Then he enters and speaks to

them, but still no reply. Finally, in anger,
he sits down at the table, and eats up all the
fish himself.[1]

Thus, it will be observed, the droll incident
which forms the subject of the old Scotch
song of "The Barring of the Door" is of
world-wide celebrity.

Gothamite stories appear to have been
familiar throughout Europe during the later
Middle Ages, if we may judge from a chapter
of the *Gesta Romanorum*, in which the
monkish compiler has curiously "moralised"
the actions of three noodles :

We read in the "Lives of the Fathers"
that an angel showed to a certain holy man
three men labouring under a triple fatuity.
The first made a faggot of wood, and because
it was too heavy for him to carry, he added
to it more wood, hoping by such means to
make it light. The second drew water with
great labour from a very deep well with
a sieve, which he incessantly filled. The
third carried a beam in his chariot, and,
wishing to enter his house, whereof the gate
was so narrow and low that it would not
admit him, he violently whipped his horse
until they both fell together into a deep well.

[1] Crane's *Italian Popular Tales*, pp. 284-5.

Having shown this to the holy man, the
angel said, "What think you of these three
men?" "That they are fools," answered he.
"Understand, however," returned the angel,
"that they represent the sinners of this world.
The first describes that kind of men who from
day to day do add new sins to the old,
because they cannot bear the weight of those
which they already have. The second man
represents those who do good, but do it
sinfully, and therefore it is of no benefit.
And the third person is he who would enter
the kingdom of heaven with all his world of
vanities, but is cast down into hell."

And now a few more Indian and other
stories of the Gothamite class to conclude
the present section. In Málava there were
two Bráhman brothers, and the wealth inherited from their father was left jointly
between them. And while they were dividing
that wealth they quarrelled about one having
too little and the other having too much, and
they made a teacher learned in the Vedas
arbitrator, and he said to them, "You must
divide everything your father left into two
halves, so that you may not quarrel about the
inequality of the division." When the two
fools heard this, they divided every single

thing into two equal parts—house, beds, in fact, all their property, including their cattle.

Henry Stephens (Henri Estienne), in the Introduction to his Apology for Herodotus,[1] relates some very amusing noodle-stories, such as of him who, burning his shins before the fire, and not having wit enough to go back from it, sent for masons to remove the chimney; of the fool who ate the doctor's prescription, because he was told to "take it ; " of another wittol who, having seen one spit upon iron to try whether it was hot, did likewise with his porridge; and, best of all, he tells of a fellow who was hit on the back with a stone as he rode upon his mule, and cursed the animal for kicking him. This last exquisite jest has its analogue in that of the Irishman who was riding on an ass one fine day, when the beast, by kicking at the flies that annoyed him, got one of its hind feet

[1] A separate work from the *Apologie pour Herodote*. Such was the exasperation of the French clerics at the bitter truths set forth in it, that the author had to flee the country. An English translation, entitled "*A World of Wonders ;* or, an Introdvction to a Treatise tovching the Conformitie of Ancient and Modern Wonders ; or, a Preparative Treatise to the 'Apologie for Herodotus,'" etc., was published at London in 1607, folio, and at Edinburgh 1608, also folio. The *Apologie pour Herodote* was printed at the Hague.

entangled in the stirrup, whereupon the rider dismounted, saying, "Faith, if you're going to get up, it's time I was getting down."

The poet Ovid alludes to the story of Ino persuading the women of the country to roast the wheat before it was sown, which may have come to India through the Greeks, since we are told in the *Kathá Sarit Ságara* of a foolish villager who one day roasted some sesame seeds, and finding them nice to eat, he sowed a large quantity of roasted seeds, hoping that similar ones would come up. The story also occurs in Coelho's *Contes Portuguezes*, and is probably of Buddhistic origin. And an analogous story is told of an Irishman who gave his hens hot water, in order that they should lay boiled eggs!

CHAPTER V.

The Silly Son.

MONG the favourite jests of all peoples, from Iceland to Japan, from India to England, are the droll adventures and mishaps of the silly son, who contrives to muddle every-thing he is set to do. In vain does his poor mother try to direct him in " the way he should go " : she gets him a wife, as a last resource ; but a fool he is still, and a fool he will always be. His blunders and disasters are chronicled in penny chap-books and in nursery rhymes, of infinite variety. Who has not heard how

> Simple Simon went a-fishing
> For to catch a whale,
> ᴜt all the water he had got
> Was in his mother's pail ?

an adventure which recalls another nursery rhyme regarding Simon's still more celebrated prototypes :

Three men of Gotham
Went to sea in a bowl;
If the bowl had been stronger,
My tale had been longer.

Then there is the prose history of *Simple Simon's Misfortunes; or, his Wife Marjory's Outrageous Cruelty*, which tells (1) of Simon's wedding, and how his wife Marjory scolded him for putting on his roast-meat clothes (*i.e.*, Sunday clothes) the very next morning after he was married; (2) how she dragged him up the chimney in a basket, a-smoke-drying, wherein they used to dry bacon, which made him look like a red herring; (3) how Simon lost a sack of corn as he was going to the mill to have it ground; (4) how Simon went to market with a basket of eggs, but broke them by the way: also how he was put into the stocks; (5) how Simon's wife cudgelled him for not bringing her money for the eggs; (6) how Simon lost his wife's pail and burnt the bottom of her kettle; (7) how Simon's wife sent him to buy two pounds of soap, but going over the bridge, he let his money fall in the river: also how a ragman ran away with his clothes. No wonder if, after this crowning misfortune, poor Simon " drank a bottle of sack, to poison himself, as being weary of his life" !

Again, we have *The Unfortunate Son; or,*

a Kind Wife is worth Gold, being full of Mirth and Pastime, which commences thus :

> There was a man but one son had,
>   And he was all his joy ;
> But still his fortune was but bad,
>   Though he was a pretty boy.
>
> His father sent him forth one day
>   To feed a flock of sheep,
> And half of them were stole away
>   While he lay down asleep !
>
> Next day he went with one Tom Goff
>   To reap as he was seen,
> When he did cut his fingers off,
>   The sickle was so keen !

Another of the chap-book histories of noodles is that of *Simple John and his Twelve Misfortunes,* an imitation of *Simple Simon ;* it was still popular amongst the rustics of Scotland fifty years ago.

The adventures of Silly Matt, the Norwegian counterpart of our typical English booby, as related in Asbjornson's collection of Norse folk-tales, furnish some curious examples of the transmission of popular fictions :

The mother of Silly Matt tells him one day that he should build a bridge across the river

and take toll of every one who wished to go
over it ; so he sets to work with a will, and
when the bridge is finished, stands at one
end—" at the receipt of custom." Three men
come up with loads of hay, and Matt demands
toll of them, so they each give him a wisp of
hay. Next comes a pedlar, with all sorts of
small wares in his pack, and Matt gets from him
two needles. On his return home his mother
asks him what he has got that day. " Hay and
needles," says Matt. Well! and what had
he done with the hay? " I put some of it in
my mouth," quoth he, " and as it tasted like
grass, I threw it into the river." She says he
ought to have spread it on the byre-floor.
" Very good," replies the dutiful Matt ; " I'll
remember that next time." And what had he
done with the needles ? He stuck them into
the hay. " Ah," says the mother, " you should
rather have stuck them in and out of your cap,
and brought them home to me." Well! well!
Matt will not forget to do so next time. The
following day a man comes to the bridge with
a sack of meal and gives Matt a pound of it ;
then comes a smith, who gives him a gimlet :
the meal he spread on the byre-floor, and the
gimlet he stuck in and out of his cap. His
mother tells him he should have come home
for a bucket to hold the meal, and the gimlet
he should have put up his sleeve. Very good !

Matt will not forget next time. Another day some men come to the bridge with kegs of brandy, of which Matt gets a pint, and pours it into his sleeve ; next comes a man driving some goats and their young ones, and gives Matt a kid, which he treads down into a bucket. His mother says he should have led the goat home with a cord round its neck, and put the brandy in a pail. Next day he gets a pat of butter and drags it home with a string. After this his mother despairs of his improvement, till it occurs to her that he might not be such a noodle if he had a wife. So she bids him go and see whether he cannot find some lass who will take him for a husband. Should he meet any folk on his way, he ought to say to them, " God's peace ! " Matt accordingly sets off in quest of a wife, and meets a she-wolf and her seven cubs. " God's peace ! " says Matt, and then returns home. When his mother learns of this, she tells him he should have cried, " Huf ! huf ! you jade wolf ! " Next day he goes off again, and meeting a bridal party, he cries, " Huf ! huf ! you jade wolf ! " and goes back to his mother and acquaints her of this fresh adventure. " O you great silly ! " says she ; " you should have said, ' Ride happily, bride and bridegroom ! '" Once more Matt sets out to seek a wife, and seeing on the road a bear taking a ride on a horse, he exclaims joyfully, "Ride happily, bride and bridegroom!" and then returns home. His mother, on hearing of this new piece of folly, tells him he should have cried, "To the devil with you!" Again he sets out, and meeting a funeral procession, he roars, "To the devil with you!" His mother says he should have cried, "May your poor soul have mercy!" and sends him off for the fifth time to look for a lass. On the road he sees some gipsies busy skinning a dead dog, upon which he piously exclaims, "May your poor soul have mercy!" His mother now goes herself to get him a wife, finds a lass that is willing to marry him, and invites her to dinner. She privately tells Matt how he should comport himself in the presence of his sweetheart; he should cast an eye at her now and then. Matt understands her instruction most literally: stealing into the sheepfold, he plucks out the eyes of all the sheep and goats, and puts them in his pocket. When he is seated beside his sweetheart, he casts a "sheep's eye" at her, which hits her on the nose.[1]

This last incident, as we have seen, occurs in the *Tales of the Men of Gotham* (*ante*, p. 41), and it is also found in a Venetian

[1] Abridged from the story of "Silly Matt" in Sir George W. Dasent's *Tales from the Fjeld.*

story (Bernoni, *Fiabe*, No. 11), entitled " The Fool," of which the following is the first part:

Once upon a time there was a mother who had a son with little brains. One morning she said, " We must get up early, for we have to make bread." So they both rose early, and began to make bread. The mother made the loaves, but took no pains to make them the same size. Her son said to her finally, "How small you have made this loaf, mother." "Oh," said she, " it does not matter whether they are big or little, for the proverb says, 'Large and small, all must go to mass.'" "Good! good!" said her son. When the bread was made, instead of taking it to the baker's, the son took it to the church, for it was the hour for mass, saying, " My mother said that, 'large and small, all must go to mass.'" So he threw the loaves down in the middle of the church. Then he went home to his mother, and said, " I have done what you told me to do." "Good! Did you take the bread to the baker's?" "O mother, if you had seen how they all looked at me!" " You might also have cast an eye on them in return," said his mother. "Wait; wait. I will cast an eye at them too," he exclaimed, and went to the stable and cut out the eyes of all the animals, and putting them in a handker-

chief, went to the church, and when any man
or woman looked at him, he threw an eye at
them.[1]

Silly Matt has a brother in Russia, according to M. Leger's *Contes Populaires Slaves*,
published at Paris in 1882: An old man and
his wife had a son, who was about as great a
noodle as could be. One day his mother said
to him, "My son, thou shouldst go about
among people, to get thyself sharpened and
rubbed down a little." "Yes, mother," says
he; "I'm off this moment." So he went to
the village, and saw two men threshing pease.
He ran up to them, and rubbed himself now
on one and then on the other. "No non-
sense!" cried the men. "Get away." But he
continued to rub himself on them, till at last
they would stand it no longer, and beat him
with their flails so lustily that he could hardly
crawl home. "What art thou crying about,
child?" asked his mother. He related his
misfortune. "Ah, my child," said she, "how
silly thou art! Thou shouldst have said to
them, 'God aid you, good men! Do you wish
me to help you to thresh?' and then they
would have given thee some pease for thy

[1] Professor Crane's *Italian Popular Tales*,
p. 302. This actual throwing of eyes occurs in
the folk-tales of Europe generally.

trouble, and we should have had them to cook
and eat." On another occasion the noodle
again went through the village, and met some
people carrying a dead man. " May God aid
you, good men !" he exclaimed. " Do you
wish me to help you to thresh ?" But he got
himself well thrashed once more for this ill-
timed speech. When he reached home, he
howled, " They've felled me to the ground,
beaten me, and plucked my beard and hair !"
and told of his new mishap. " Ah, noodle !"
said his mother, " thou shouldst have said,
' God give peace to his soul !' Thou shouldst
have taken off thy bonnet, wept, and fallen
upon thy knees. They would then have given
thee meat and drink." Again he went to the
village, and met a marriage procession. So
he took off his bonnet, and cried with all his
might, " God grant peace to his soul !" and
then burst into tears. " What brute is this ?"
said the wedding company. " We laugh and
amuse ourselves, and he laments as if he were
at a funeral." So they leaped out of the car-
riages, and beat him soundly on the ribs.
Home he returned, crying, " They've beaten
me, thrashed me, and torn my beard and
hair !" and related what had happened. " My
son," said his mother, " thou shouldst have
leaped and danced with them." The next
time he went to the village he took his bag-

9

pipe under his arm.   At the end of the street
a cart-shed was on fire.   The noodle ran to
the spot, and began to play on his bagpipe
and to dance and caper about, for which he
was abused as before.   Going back to his
mother in tears, he told her how he had fared.
"My son," said she, "thou shouldst have
carried water and thrown it on the fire, like
the other folks."   Three days later, when his
ribs were well again, the noodle went through
the village once more, and seeing a man roast-
ing a little pig, he seized a vessel of water,
ran up with it, and threw the water on the
fire.   This time also he was beaten, and when
he got home, and told his mother of his ill-
luck, she resolved never again to allow him to
go abroad ; so he remains by the fireside, as
great a fool as ever.

This species of noodle is also known in
Japan.   He is the hero of a farce entitled
Hone Kaha, or Ribs and Skin, which has
been done into English by Mr. Basil Hall
Chamberlain, in his *Classical Poetry of the
Japanese*. The rector of a Buddhist temple tells
his curate that he feels he is now getting too
old for the duties of his office, and means to
resign the benefice in his favour.   Before re-
tiring to his private chamber, he desires the
curate to let him know if any persons visit

the temple, and bids him, should he be in
want of information regarding any matter, to
come to him. A parishioner calls to borrow an
umbrella. The curate lends him a new one, and
then goes to the rector and informs him of this
visitor. "You have done wrong," says the rector.
"You ought to have said that you should
have been happy to comply with such a small
request, but, unfortunately, the rector was
walking out with it the other day, when, at a
place where four roads meet, a sudden gust
of wind blew the skin to one side and the
ribs to another; we have tied the ribs and
skin together in the middle, and hung it from
the ceiling. Something like that," adds the
rector, "something with an air of truth about
it, is what you should have said." Next comes
another parishioner, who wishes to borrow a
horse. The curate replies with great polite-
ness, "The request with which you honour
me is a mere trifle, but the rector took it out
with him a few days since, and coming to the
junction of four cross roads, a gust of wind
blew the ribs to one side and the skin to
another, and we have tied them together, and
hung them from the ceiling; so I fear it would
not suit your purpose." "It is a horse I want,"
said the man. "Precisely—a horse: I am
aware of it," quoth the curate, and the man
went off, not a little perplexed, after which

the curate reports this new affair to the rector, who says it was to an umbrella, not to a horse, that such a story was applicable. Should any one come again to borrow a horse, he ought to say, "I much regret that I cannot comply with your request. The fact is, we lately turned him out to grass, and becoming frolicsome, he dislocated his thigh, and is now lying, covered with straw, in a corner of the stable." "Something like that," adds the rector, "something with an air of truth about it, is what you should say." A third parishioner comes to invite the rector and the curate to a feast at his house. "For myself," says the curate, "I promise to come ; but I fear it will not be convenient for the rector to accompany me." "I presume then," says the man, "that he has some particular business on hand?" "No, not any particular business," answers the curate ; "but the truth is, we lately turned him out to grass, and becoming frisky, he dislocated his thigh, and now lies in a corner of the stable, covered with straw." "I spoke of the rector," says the parishioner. "Yes, of the rector. I quite understand," responds the curate, very complaisantly, upon which the man goes away, not knowing what to make of such a strange account of the rector's condition. This last affair puts the rector into a fury, and he cuffs his intended successor, exclaiming,

"When was I ever frisky, I should like to know?"

As great a jolterhead as any of the foregoing was the hero of a story in Cazotte's "Continuation" of the *Arabian Nights*, entitled "L'Imbécille; ou, L'Histoire de Xailoun." This noodle's wife said to him one day, "Go and buy some pease, and don't forget that it is pease you are to buy; continually repeat 'Pease!' till you reach the market-place." So he went off, with "Pease! pease!" always in his mouth. He passed the corner of a street where a merchant who had pearls for sale was proclaiming his wares in a loud voice, saying, "In the name of the Prophet, pearls!" Xailoun's attention was at once attracted by the display of pearls, and at the same time he was occupied in retaining the lesson his wife had taught him, and putting his hand in

---

[1] In *Le Cabinet des Fées*, 1788 (tome xxxviii., p. 337 ff.).—There can be no such name as Xailoun in Arabic; that of the noodle's wife, Oitba, may be intended for "Utba." Cazotte has so Frenchified the names of the characters in his tales as to render their identification with the Arabic originals (where he had any such) often impossible. Although this story is not found in any known Arabian text of the *Book of the Thousand and One Nights*, yet the incidents for the most part occur in several Eastern story-books.

the box of pearls, he cried out, "Pease!
pease!" The merchant, supposing Xailoun
played upon him and depreciated his pearls
by wishing to make them pass for false ones,
struck him a severe blow. "Why do you
strike me?" said Xailoun. "Because you
insult me," answered the merchant. "Do you
suppose I am trying to deceive people?"
"No," said the noodle. "But what must I say,
then?" "If you will cry properly, say as I
do, 'Pearls, in the name of the Prophet!'"
He next passed by the shop of a merchant
from whom some pearls had been stolen, and
his manner of crying, "Pearls!" etc., which
was not nearly so loud as usual, appeared to the
merchant very suspicious. "The man who has
stolen my pearls," thought he, "has probably
recognised me, and when he passes my shop
lowers his voice in crying the goods." Upon
this suspicion he ran after Xailoun, and stop-
ping him, said, "Show me your pearls." The
poor fool was in great confusion, and the
merchant thought he had got the thief. The
supposed seller of pearls was soon surrounded
by a great crowd, and the merchant at last
discovered that he was a perfect simpleton.
"Why," said he, "do you cry that you sell
pearls?" "What should I say, then?" asked
Xailoun. "It is not true," said the merchant,
not listening to him. "It is not true,"

exclaimed the noodle. "**Let me** repeat, ' It is not true,' that I may not forget it ; " and as he went on he kept crying, " It is not true." His way led him towards a place where a man was proclaiming, " In the name of the Prophet, lentils !" Xailoun, induced by curiosity, went up to the man, his mouth full of the last words he remembered, and putting his hand into the sack, cried, " It is not true." The sturdy villager gave him a blow that caused him to stagger, saying, " What d'ye mean by giving me the lie about my goods, which I both sowed and reaped myself ? " Quoth the noodle, " I have only tried to say what I ought to say." " Well, then," rejoined the dealer, " you ought to say, as I do, ' Lentils, in the name of the Prophet !' " So our noodle at once took up this new cry, and proceeded on his way till he came to the bank of the river, where a fisherman had been casting his net for hours, and had frequently changed his place, without getting any fish. Xailoun, who was amused with every new thing he saw, began to follow the fisherman, and, that he should not forget his lesson, continued to repeat, " Lentils, in the name of the Prophet !" Suddenly the fisherman made a pretence of spreading his net, in order to wring and dry it, and having folded in his hand the rope to which it was fastened, he took hold

of the simpleton and struck him some furious
blows with it, saying, "Vile sorcerer! cease
to curse my fishing." Xailoun struggled, and
at length disengaged himself. "I am no
sorcerer," said he. "Well, if you are not,"
answered the fisherman, "why do you cause
me bad luck by your words every time I throw
my net?" "I didn't mean to bring you bad
luck," said the noodle. "I only repeat what
I was told to repeat." The fisherman then
concluded that some of his enemies, who
wished to do him an ill turn without expos-
ing themselves, had prevailed upon this poor
fellow to come and curse his fishing, so he
said, "I am sorry, brother, for having beaten
you, but you were wrong to pronounce the
words you did, thereby bringing bad luck to
me, who never did you any harm." Quoth
the simpleton, "I only tried to say the words
my wife told me not to forget." "Do you
know them?" "Yes." "Well, place yourself beside me, and each time I cast my net
you must say, 'In the name of the Prophet,
instead of one, seven of the greatest and
best!'" But Xailoun thought what his wife
had said was not so long as that. "Oh, yes,
it was," said the fisherman; "and take care
you don't miss a single word, and I shall give
you some of the fish to take home with you."
That he might not forget, Xailoun repeated it

very loud, but as he was afraid of the cord whenever he saw the fisherman drawing in his net, he ran away as fast as he could, but still repeating, "In the name of the Prophet, instead of one, seven of the greatest and best!" These words he pronounced in the midst of a crowd of people, through which the corpse of the kází (magistrate, or judge) was being carried to the burying ground, and the mullahs who surrounded the bier, scandalised by what they thought a horrible imprecation, exclaimed, "How darest thou, wicked wretch, thus blaspheme? Is it not enough that Death has taken one of the greatest men of Baghdád?" The poor simpleton was skulking off in fear and trembling, when his sleeve was pulled by an aged slave, who told him that he ought to say, "May Allah preserve his body and save his soul!" So our noodle went on, repeating this new cry till he came to a street where a dead ass was being carted away. "May Allah preserve his body and save his soul!" he exclaimed. "How he blasphemes!" said the folk, and they set upon him with their fists and sticks, and gave him a sound drubbing. At length he got clear of them, and by chance came to the house of his wife's mother, but he only ventured to stand at the door and peep within. He was recognised, however, and asked what he

would have to eat—goat's flesh ? rice ? *pease ?*
Yes, it was pease he wanted, and having got
some, he hastened home, and after relating
all his mishaps, informed his wife, that her
sister was very sick. His wife, having prepared herself to go to her mother's house,
tells the simpleton to rock the baby should it
awake and cry; feed the hen that was sitting;
if the ass was thirsty, give her to drink; shut
the door, and take care not to go to sleep, lest
robbers should come and plunder the house.
The baby awakes, and Xailoun rocks it to sleep
again; so far, well. The hen seems uneasy;
he concludes she is troubled with insects, like
himself. So he takes up the hen, and thinking the best way to kill the insects was to
stick a pin into them, he unluckily kills the
hen. This was a serious matter, and while
he considers what he should do in the circumstances, the ass begins to bray. "Ah," says
he, "I've no time to attend to you just now;
but when I am on your back, you can carry
me to the river." Then he opened the door
and let out the ass and her colt. After this
he sat down on the eggs, and took the baby
in his arms. His wife returning, knocks at
the door. "Let me in, you fool," she cries.
"I can't, for I am nursing the baby and hatch-
ing the eggs." At length she contrived to
force open the door, and running up to her

idiot of a husband, fetched him a blow that caused him to crush all the half-hatched eggs. Luckily she had met the ass and her foal on the road, so the amount of mischief done by her stupid spouse in her absence was not so great, all things considered.[1]

The misadventures of the Arabian idiot in his expedition to purchase pease present a close analogy to those of the typical English booby, only the latter end tragically :

A woman sent her son one day to buy a sheep's head and pluck, and, lest he should forget his message, he kept bawling loudly as he went along, "Sheep's head and pluck! sheep's head and pluck!" In getting over a stile he fell and hurt himself, and forgot what he was sent for, so he stood a little to consider ; and at last he thought he recollected

---

[1] On a similar occasion Giufà, the Sicilian brother to the Arabian fool, did somewhat more mischief. Once his mother went to church and told him to make some porridge for his baby-sister. Giufà made a great pot of porridge and fed the baby with it, and burned her mouth so that she died. Another time his mother on leaving home told him to feed the hen that was sitting and put her back in the nest, so that the eggs should not get cold. Giufà stuffed the hen with food so that he killed her, and then sat on the eggs himself until his mother returned.—See Crane's *Italian Popular Tales*, pp. 296-7.

it, and began to shout, "Liver and lights and gall and all!" which he was repeating when he came up to a man who was very sick. The man, thinking the booby was mocking him, laid hold of him, and after cuffing him, bade the booby cry, "Pray God, send no more up!" So he ran along uttering these words till he came to a field where a man was sowing wheat, who, on hearing what he took for a curse upon his labour, seized and thrashed him, and told him to repeat, "Pray God, send plenty more!" So the young jolterhead at once "changed his tune," and was loudly singing out these words when he met a funeral. The chief mourner punished him for what he thought his fiendish wish, and bade him say, "Pray God, send the soul to heaven!" which he was bawling when he met a he and a she-dog going to be hanged. The good people who heard him were greatly shocked at his seeming profanity, and striking him, strictly charged him to cry, "A he and a she-dog going to be hanged!" On he went, accordingly, repeating this new cry, till he met a man and a woman going to be married. When the bridegroom heard what the booby said, he gave him many a good thump, and bade him say, "I wish you much joy!" This he was crying at the top of his voice when he came to a pit into which two labourers had fallen, and one of them, enraged at what he thought his mockery of their misfortune, exerted all his strength and scrambled out, then beat the poor simpleton, and told him to say, " The one is out , I wish the other was ! " Glad to be set free, the booby went on shouting these words till he met with a one-eyed man, who, like the others, taking what he was crying for a personal insult, gave him another drubbing, and then bade him cry, " The one side gives good light, and I wish the other did ! " So he adopted this new cry, and continued his adventurous journey till he came to a house, one side of which was on fire. The people, hearing him bawling, " The one side gives good light, and I wish the other did ! " at once concluded that he had set the house a-blazing; so they put him in prison, and the end was, the judge put on the black cap and condemned him to be hanged ! [1]

When the noodle is persuaded, as in the following case of a Sinhalese wittol, by a gang of thieves to join them in a plundering expedition, they have little reason to be pleased with him, for he does not make a

[1] Abridged and modified from a version in the *Folk-Lore Record*, vol. iii., pp. 153-5.

good "cat's-paw."   The Sinhalese noodle joined some thieves, took readily to their ways, and was always eager to accompany them on their marauding excursions.   One night they took him with them, and boring a large hole in the wall of a house,[1] they sent him in, telling him to hand out the heaviest article he could lay hands upon.   He readily went in, and seeing a large kurakkan-grinder,[2] thought that was the heaviest thing in the room, and attempted to remove it.   But it proved too much for him alone, so he gently awoke a man who was sleeping in the room, and said to him, "My friend, pray help me to remove this kurakkan-grinder." The man immediately guessed that thieves had entered the house, and gave the alarm. The thieves, who were waiting outside quite expectant, rushed away, and the noodle somehow or other managed to escape with them.

Next night they again took him along with them, and after boring a hole in the wall of another house, sent him in with strict injunctions not to make a noise or wake anybody. He crept in noiselessly and entered a large

[1] The usual mode by which in the East thieves break into houses, which are for the most part constructed of clay.   See Job xxiv. 16.

[2] Kurakkan is a species of grain.

room, in which was an old woman, fast asleep by the fire, with wide-open mouth. An earthen chattie, a wooden spoon, and a small bag of pease were also placed by the fire. The noodle first proceeded to roast some pease in the chattie. When they were roasted to a nice brownish colour, and emitted a very tempting smell, he thought that the old woman might also enjoy a mouthful. He considered for a while how he might best offer some to her. He did not wish to wake her, as he was ordered not to wake anybody. Suddenly a bright idea struck him. Why should he not feed her? There she was sleeping with her mouth wide open. Surely it would be no difficult task to put some pease into her mouth. Taking some of the hot, smoking pease into the wooden spoon, he put the contents into her mouth. The woman awoke, screaming with all her might. The noise roused the other inmates of the house, who came rushing to the spot to see what was the matter. This time also the noodle managed to escape with the thieves; but in a subsequent adventure he, as well as the thieves, came to grief.[1]

The silly son of Italian popular tales is

[1] *The Orientalist*, June, 1884, pp. 137-8.

represented as being sent by his mother to sell a piece of linen which she had woven, saying to him, "Now listen attentively to what I say: Walk straight along the road. Don't take less than such a price for this linen. Don't have any dealings with women who chatter. Whether you sell it to any one you meet on the way, or carry it into the market, offer it only to some quiet sort of body whom you may see standing apart and not gossiping or prating, for such as they will persuade you to take some sort of price that won't suit me at all." The booby answers. "Yes, mamma," and goes off on his errand, keeping straight on, instead of taking the turnings leading to villages. It happened, as he went along, that the wife of the syndic of the next town was driving out with her maids, and had got out of the carriage, to walk a short distance, as the day was fine. Her maid tells her that there goes the simple son of the poor widow by the brook. "What are you going to do, my good lad?" kindly asks the lady. "I'm not going to tell you," says the booby, "because you were chattering." "I see your mother has sent you to sell this linen," continues the lady; "I will buy it of you," and she offers to pay twice as much as his mother had said she wanted. "Can't sell it to you," replies he, "for you

were chattering," and he continues his
journey. Farther along he comes to a plaster
statue by the roadside, so he says to himself,
"Here's one who stands apart and doesn't
chatter; this is the one to sell the linen to,"
then aloud, "Will you buy my linen, good
friend?" The statue maintained its usual
taciturnity, and the booby concluded, as it
did not speak, it was all right, so he said,
"The price is so-and-so; have the money
ready by the time I come back, as I have to
go on and buy some yarn for mother." On
he went accordingly, and bought the yarn,
and then came back to the statue. Some one
passing by had in the meantime taken the
linen. Finding it gone, "It's all right," says
he to himself; "she's taken it," then aloud,
"Where's the money I told you to have
ready?" The statue remained silent. "If
you don't give me the money, I'll hit you on
the head," he exclaimed, and raising his stick,
he knocked the head off, and found it filled
with gold coin. "That's where you keep
your money, is it? All right; I can pay myself." So saying, he filled his pockets with the
coin and went home. When he handed his
mother the money, and told her of his adventure with the quiet body by the roadside, she
was afraid lest the neighbours should learn
of her windfall if the booby knew its value

so she said to him, "You've only brought me
a lot of rusty nails; but never mind: you'll
know better what to do next time," and put
the money in an earthen jar. In her absence,
a ragman comes to the house, and the booby
asks him, "Will you buy some rusty nails?"
The man desires to see them. "Well,"
quoth he on beholding the treasure, "they're
not much worth, but I'll give you twelve
pauls for the lot," and having handed over
the sum, went off with his prize. When his
mother comes home, the booby tells her
what a bargain he had made for the rusty
nails. "Nails!" she echoes, in consternation.
"Why, you foolish thing, they were gold
coins!" "Can't help that now, mamma," he
answers philosophically; "you told me they
were old rusty nails." By another lucky
adventure, however, the booby is enabled to
make up his mother's loss, finding a treasure
which a party of robbers had left behind
them at the foot of a tree.

The incident of a simpleton selling something to an inanimate object and discovering
a hidden treasure occurs, in different forms,
in the folk-tales of Asiatic as well as
European countries. In a manuscript text of
the *Arabian Nights*, brought from Constan-
tinople by Wortley Montague, and now

preserved in the Bodleian Library, Oxford, a more elaborate version of the Italian booby's adventure with the statue is found, in the "Story of the Bang-eater and his Wife:"

In former itimes there lived not far from Baghdád a half-witted fellow, who was much addicted to the use of bang. Being reduced to poverty, he was obliged to sell his cow, which he took to the market one day, but the animal being in such a poor condition, no one would buy it, and after waiting till he was weary he returned homeward. On the way he stopped to repose himself under a tree, and tied the cow to one of the branches, while he ate some bread, and drank an infusion of his bang, which he always carried with him. In a short time it began to operate, so as to bereave him of the little sense he had, and his head was filled with ridiculous reveries. While he was musing, a bird beginning to chatter from her nest in the tree, he fancied it was a human voice, and that some woman had offered to purchase his cow, upon which he said, "Reverend mother of Solomon,[1] dost thou wish to buy my

[1] Ummu Sulayman. In Arabia the mother is generally addressed in this way as a mark of respect for having borne children, and the eldest gives the title. Our bang-eater supposed he was addressing an old woman who had (or might have had) a son named Solomon.

cow?" The bird again chatteied. "Well,"
replied he, "what wilt thou give? I will
sell her a bargain." The bird repeated her
noise. "Never mind," said the fool, "for
though thou hast forgotten to bring thy purse,
yet, as I daresay thou art an honest woman,
and hast bidden me ten dînars, I will trust
thee with the cow, and call on Friday for the
money." The bird renewed her chattering;
so, leaving the cow tied to a branch of the
tree, he returned home, exulting in the good
bargain he had made for the animal. When
he entered the house, his wife inquired what
he had got for the cow, and he replied that
he had sold her to an honest woman, who
had promised to pay him ten pieces of gold
next Friday. The wife was contented; and
when Friday arrived, her noodle of a husband
having, as usual, taken a dose of bang, repaired
to the tree, and hea.ing the bird chattering as
before, said, "Well, good mother, hast thou
brought the gold?" The bird croaked. The
blockhead, supposing the imaginary woman
refused to pay him, became angry, and threw
up a stone, which frightening the bird, it flew
from its nest in the tree and alighted on a
heap of ruins at some little distance. He
now concluded that the woman had desired
him to take his money from the heap, into
which he accordingly dug, and found a copper

vessel full of coin. This discovery convinced him he was right, and being withal an honest fellow, he only took ten pieces; then replacing the soil, " May Allah requite thee for thy punctuality, good mother!" he exclaimed, and returned to his wife, to whom he gave the money, informing her at the same time of the great treasure his friend the imaginary old woman possessed, and where it was concealed.

The wife waited till night, when she brought away the pot of gold, which her foolish husband observing, he said, " It is dishonest to rob one who has paid us so punctually; and if thou dost not return it to its place, I will inform the wali " (governor of the city). She laughed at his simplicity, but fearing that he would execute his threat, she planned a stratagem to render it of no avail. Going to market, she purchased some meat and fish ready cooked, which she brought privately home, and concealed in the house. At night, while her husband was sleeping off the effects of his favourite narcotic, she strewed the provisions she had brought outside the door, and then awakening him, cried out, " Dear husband, a most wonderful thing has occurred : there has been a violent storm while you slept, and, strange to tell, it has rained pieces of broiled meat and fish, which now lie at the door!" The blockhead got up, and seeing the food, was persuaded of the truth of his wife's story. The flesh and fish were gathered up, and he partook with much glee of the miraculous treat, but still said he would tell the walí of her having stolen the treasure of the honest old woman.

In the morning he actually repaired to the walí, and informed him that his wife had stolen a pot of gold, which she had still in her possession. Upon this the walí had the woman apprehended. She denied the accusation, and was then threatened with death. "My lord," said she, "the power is in your hands; but I am an injured woman, as you will find by questioning my husband, who is deranged in his intellect. Ask him when I committed the theft." The walí did so, and the simpleton answered, "It was the evening of that night when it rained broiled fish and ready-cooked flesh." On hearing this, "Wretch!" exclaimed the walí in a fury, "dost thou dare to utter falsehoods before me? Who ever saw it rain anything but water?" "As I hope for life," replied the fool, "I speak the truth; for my wife and myself ate of the fish and flesh which fell from the clouds." The woman, being appealed to, denied the assertion of her husband. The walí, now convinced that the man was crazy, released the woman, and sent her husband to the madhouse, where he remained for some days, till his wife, pitying his condition, contrived to get him set at liberty. She visited her husband, and counselled him, should any one ask him if he had seen it rain fish and flesh, to answer, "No; who ever saw it rain anything but water?" Then she informed the keeper that he was come to his senses, and suggested he should question him; and on the poor fellow answering properly he was released.

In a Russian variant, an old man had three sons, one of whom was a noodle. When the old man died, his property was shared between the brothers, but all that the simpleton received was one ox, which he took to the market to sell. On his way he chanced to pass an old birch-tree, which creaked and groaned in the wind. He thinks the tree is offering to buy his ox, and so he says, "Well, you shall have it for twenty roubles." But the tree only creaked and creaked, and he fancied it was asking the ox on credit. "Very good," says he. "You'll pay me to-morrow? I'll wait till then." So he ties the ox to the tree and goes home. His brothers question him about his ox, and he tells them he has sold it for twenty roubles and is to get

the money to-morrow, at which they laugh;
he is, they think, a greater fool than ever.
Next morning he went to the birch-tree, and
found the ox was gone, for, in truth, the
wolves had eaten it. He demanded his money,
but the tree only creaked and groaned, as
usual. " You'll pay me to-morrow ? " he
exclaimed. " That's what you said yesterday.
I'll have no more of your promises." So
saying, he struck the old birch-tree with his
hatchet and sent the chips flying about. Now
the tree was hollow, and it soon split asunder
from his blows; and in the hollow trunk he
found a pot full of gold, which some robbers
had hidden there. Taking some of the gold,
he returns home, and shows it to his brothers,
who ask him how he got so much money.
"A neighbour," he replies, " gave it to me for
my ox. But this is nothing like the whole of
it. Come along, brothers, and let us get the
rest." They go, and fetch the rest of the
treasure, and on their way home they meet a
diachok (one of the inferior members of the
Russian clerical body, though not one of the
clergy), who asks them what they are carrying. " Mushrooms," say the two clever
brothers; but the noodle cries, " That's not
true; we're carrying money: here, look at it."
The diachok, with an exclamation, flung himself upon the gold and began stuffing it into

his pockets. At this the noodle grew angry, dealt him a blow with his hatchet, and killed him on the spot. The brothers dragged the body to an empty cellar, and flung it in. Later in the evening the eldest said to the other, "This business is sure to turn out badly. When they look for the diachok, Simpleton will be sure to tell them all about it. So we had better hide the body in some other place, and kill a goat and bury it in the cellar." This they did accordingly. And after several days had passed the people asked the noodle if he had seen the diachok. "Yes," he answered. "I killed him some time ago with my hatchet, and my brothers carried him to the cellar." They seize upon him and compel him to go down into the cellar and bring out the body. He gets hold of the goat's head, and asks, "Was your diachok dark-haired?" "He was." "Had he a beard?" "Yes." "And horns?" "What horns are you talking of?" "Well, see for yourselves," said he, tossing up the head to them. They saw it was a goat's head, and went away home.[1]

The reader cannot fail to remark the close resemblance there is between the first parts

[1] See Ralston's *Russian Folk-Tales.*

of the Arabian and Russian stories; and the second parts of both reappear in many tales of the Silly Son. The goat's carcase substituted for the dead man occurs, for instance, in the Norse story of Silly Matt; in the Sicilian story of Giufà; in M. Rivière's *Contes Populaires de la Kabylie du Djurdjura;* and "Foolish Sachûli," in Miss Stokes' *Indian Fairy Tales.* The incident of the pretended shower of broiled fish and flesh is found in Campbell's *Tales of the West Highlands* (porridge and pancakes); in Rivière's Tales of the Kabaïl (fritters); "Foolish Sachûli" (sweetmeats); Giufà, the Sicilian Booby (figs and raisins); and in M. Leger's *Contes Populaires Slaves,* where, curiously enough, the trick is played by a husband upon his wife. It is perhaps worth while reproducing the Russian story from Leger, in a somewhat abridged form, as follows:

In tilling the ground a labourer found a treasure, and carrying it home, said to his wife, "See! Heaven has sent us a fortune. But where can we conceal it?" She suggested he should bury it under the floor, which he did accordingly. Soon after this the wife went out to fetch water, and the labourer reflected that his wife was a dreadful gossip, and by to-morrow night all the village would know their secret. So he removed the treasure from its hiding-place and buried it in his barn, beneath a heap of corn. When the wife came back from the well, he said to her quite gravely, " To-morrow we shall go to the forest to seek fish; they say there's plenty there at present." " What! fish in the forest? she exclaimed. " Of course," he rejoined ; " and you'll see them there." Very early next morning he got up, and took some fish, which he had concealed in a basket. He went to the grocer's and bought a quantity of sweet cakes. He also caught a hare and killed it. The fish and cakes he disposed of in different parts of the wood, and the hare he hooked on a fishing-line, and then threw it in the river. After breakfast he took his wife with him into the wood, which they had scarcely entered when she found a pike, then a perch, and then a roach, on the ground. With many exclamations of surprise, she gathered up the fish and put them in her basket. Presently they came to a pear-tree, from the branches of which hung sweet cakes. " See !" she cried. " Cakes on a pear-tree !" " Quite natural," replied he: "it has rained cakes, and some have remained on this tree ; travellers have picked up the rest." Continuing their way to the village, they passed near a stream. " Wait a little," said the husband ; " I set my line early this morning, and I'll look if anything is caught on it." He then pulled in the line, and behold, there was a hare hooked on to it! "How extraordinary!" cries the good wife—"a hare in the water!" "Why," says he, " don't you know there are hares in the water as well as rats?" "No, indeed, I knew it not." They now returned home, and the wife set about preparing all the nice eatables for supper. In a day or two the labourer found from the talk of his acquaintances that his finding the treasure was no secret in the village, and in less than a week he was summoned to the castle. "Is it true," said the lord, "that you have found a treasure?" "It is not true," was his reply. "But your wife has told me all." "My wife does not know what she says—she is mad, my lord." Hereupon the woman cries, "It is the truth, my lord ; he has found a treasure and buried it beneath the floor of our cottage." "When?" "On the eve before the day we went into the forest to look for fish." "What do you say?" "Yes; it was on the day that it rained cakes; we gathered a basketful of them, and coming home, my husband fished a fine hare out of the river." My lord declared the woman to be an idiot; nevertheless he caused his servants to search under the labourer's cottage floor, but nothing was found there, and so the shrewd fellow secured his treasure.

The silly son figures frequently in Indian story-books; sometimes a number of fools' exploits are strung together and ascribed to one individual, as in the tale of "Foolish Sachúli;" but generally they are told as separate stories. The following adventure of Sachúli is also found, in varied form, in Beschi's *Gooroo Paramartan:* One day Sachúli climbed up a tree, and sat on a long branch, and began cutting off the branch between the tree and himself. A man passing by called to him, saying, "What are you doing up there? You will be killed if you cut that branch off." "What do you say?" asked the booby, coming down. "When shall I die?" "How can I tell?" said the man. "Let me go." "I will not let you go until you tell me when I shall die." At last the man, in order to get rid of him, said, "When you find a scarlet thread on your jacket, then you will die." After this Sachúli went to the bazaar, and sat down by some tailors, and in throwing away shreds, a scarlet thread fell on his clothes. "Now I shall die!" exclaimed the fool. "How do you know that?" the tailors inquired, when he told them what the man had said about a scarlet thread, at which they all laughed. Nevertheless, Sachúli went and dug a grave in the jungle and lay down in it.

Presently a sepoy comes along, bearing a pot of *ghí*, or clarified butter, which he engages Sachúli to carry for him, and the noodle, of course, lets it fall in the midst of his calculations of the uses to which he should put the money he is promised by the sepoy.

The incident of a blockhead cutting off the branch on which he is seated seems to be almost universal. It occurs in the jests of the typical Turkish noodle, the Khoja Nasr-ed-Dín, and there exist German, Saxon, and Lithuanian variants of the same story. It is also known in Ceylon, and the following is a version from a Hindú work entitled *Bharataka Dwátrinsati*, Thirty-two Tales of Mendicant Monks:

In Elákapura there lived several mendicant monks. One of them, named Dandaka, once went, in the rainy season, into a wood in order to procure a post for his hut. There he saw on a tree a fine branch bent down, and he climbed the tree, sat on the branch, and began to cut it. Then there came that way some travellers, who, seeing what he was doing, said, "O monk, greatest of all idiots, you should not cut a branch on which you yourself are sitting, for if you do so, when the branch breaks you will fall down and die." After saying this the travellers went their way. The monk, however, paid no attention to their speech, but continued to cut the branch, remaining in the same posture, until at length the branch broke, and he tumbled down. He then thought within himself, "Those travellers are indeed wise and truthful, for everything has happened just as they predicted; consequently I must be dead." So he remained on the ground as if dead; he did not speak, nor did he stand up, nor did he even breathe. People who came there from the neighbourhood raised him up, but he did not stand; they endeavoured to make him speak, but could not succeed. They then sent word to the other monks, saying, "Your associate Dandaka fell down from a tree and died." Then came the monks in large numbers, and when they saw that he was "dead," they lifted him up in order to carry him to the place of cremation. Now when they had gone a short distance they came upon a spot where the road divided itself before them. Then said some, "We must go to the left," but others said, "It is to the right that we must go." Thus a dispute arose among them, and they were unable to come to any conclusion. The "dead" monk, who was borne on a bier, said, "Friends, quarrel not among yourselves; when I was alive, I always went by the left road." Then said some, "He always spoke the truth; all that he ever said was nothing but the simple fact. Let us therefore take the left road." This was agreed upon, and as they were about to proceed towards the left some people who happened to be present said, "O ye monks, ye are the greatest of all blockheads that ye should proceed to burn this man while he is yet alive." They answered, "Nay, but he is dead." Then the bystanders said, "He cannot be dead, seeing that he yet speaks." They then set down the bier on the ground, and Dandaka persistently declared that he was actually dead, and related to them with the most solemn protestations the prediction of the travellers, and how it was fulfilled. Hereupon the other monks remained quite bewildered, unable to arrive at any decision as to whether Dandaka was dead or alive, until at length, after a great deal of trouble, the bystanders succeeded in convincing them that the man was not dead and in inducing them to return to their dwelling. Dandaka also now stood up and went his way, after having been heartily laughed at by the people.[1]

A diverting story in the *Facetiæ* of Poggius, entitled "Mortuus Loqueus," from which it was reproduced in the Italian novels of

[1] From a paper on "Comparative Folk-lore," by W. Goonetilleke. in *The Orientalist,* i., p. 122.

Grazzini and in our old collection *Tales and Quicke Answeres*, has a near affinity with jests of this class, and also with the wide cycle of stories in which a number of rogues combine to cheat a simpleton out of his property. In the early English jest-book,[1] it is, in effect, as follows :

There once dwelt in Florence a noodle called Nigniaca, upon whom a party of young men resolved to play a practical joke. Having arranged their plans, one of them met him early one morning, and asked him if he was not ill. "No," says the wittol. "I am well enough." "By my faith," quoth the joker, "but you have a pale, sickly colour," and went his way. Presently a second of the complotters came up to him, and asked him if he was not suffering from an ague, for he certainly looked very ill. The poor fellow now began to think that he was really sick, and was convinced of this when a third man in passing told him that he should be in his bed—he had evidently not an hour to live. Hearing this, Nigniaca stood stock-still, saying to himself, "Verily, I have some sharp ague," when a fourth man came and bade him go home at once, for he was a dying man.

[1] *Mery Tales, Wittie Questions, and Quicke Answeres, very pleasant to be Readde.* Imprinted at London by H. Wykes, 1567.

II

So the simpleton begged this fourth man to help him home, which he did very willingly, and after laying him in his bed, the other jokers came to see him, and one of them, pretending to be a physician, felt his pulse and declared the patient would die within an hour.[1] Then, standing all about his bed, they said to each other, " Now he is sinking fast; his speech and sight have failed him; he will soon give up the ghost. Let us there- fore close his eyes, cross his hands on his breast, and carry him forth to be buried." The simpleton lay as still as though he was really dead, so they laid him on a bier and carried him through the city. A great crowd soon gathered, when it was known that they were carrying the corpse of Nigniaca to his grave. And among the crowd was a taverner's boy, who cried out, " What a rascal and thief

---

[1] Thus, too, Scogin and his "chamber-fellow" successively declared to a rustic that the sheep he was driving were pigs. In Fortini's novels, in like manner, a simpleton is persuaded that the kid he offered for sale was a capon; and in the Spanish *El Conde Lucanor,* and the German *Tyl Eulenspiegel,* a countryman is cheated out of a piece of cloth. The original form of the inci- dent is found in the *Hitopadesa,* where three sharpers persuade a Bráhman that the goat he is carrying for a sacrifice is a dog. This story of the Florentine noodle—or rather Poggio's version —may have been suggested by a tale in the

is dead ! By the mass, he should have been
hanged long ago." When the wittol heard
himself thus vilified, he lifted up his head and
exclaimed, " I wish, you scoundrel, I were
alive now, as I am dead, and I would prove
thee a false liar to thy face ; " upon which the
jokers burst into laughter, set down the
" body " and ran away—leaving Nigniaca to
explain the whole affair to the marvelling
multitude.[1]

We read of another silly son, in the *Kathá
Manjari*, whose father said to him one day,
" My boy, you are now grown big, yet you

Gesta Romanorum, in which the emperor's
physician is made to believe that he had leprosy.
See my *Popular Tales and Fictions*, where these
and similar stories are compared in a paper
entitled "The Sharpers and the Simpleton."

[1] In Powell and Magnusson's *Legends of Iceland*
(Second Series, p. 627), a woman makes her
husband believe that he is dressed in fine clothes
when he is naked ; another persuades her husband that he is dead, and as he is being carried
to the burying-ground, he perceives the naked
man, who asserts that he is dressed, upon which
he exclaims, "How I should laugh if I were not
dead ! " And in a *fabliau* by Jean de Boves, "Le
Villain de Bailleul ; *aliàs*, Le Femme qui fit
croire à son Mari qu'il était mort," the husband
exclaims, "Rascal of a priest, you may well
thank Heaven that I am dead, else I would
belabour you soundly with my stick."—See
M. Le Grand's *Fabliaux*, ed. 1781, tome v., pp.
192, 193.

don't seem to have much sense. You must, however, do something for your living. Go, therefore, to the tank, and catch fish and bring them home." The lad accordingly went to the tank, and having caused all the water —which was required for the irrigation of his father's fields—to run to waste, he picked up from the mud all the fishes he could find, and took them to his father, not a little proud of his exploit.—In the *Kathá Sarit Ságara* it is related that a Bráhman told his foolish son one evening that he must send him to the village early on the morrow, and thither the lad went, without asking what he was to do. Returning home at night very tired, he said to his father, " I have been to the village." "Yes," said the Bráhman, "you went thither without an object, and have done no good by it."—And in the Buddhist *Játakas* we find what is probably the original of a world-wide story : A man was chopping a felled tree, when a mosquito settled on his bald head and stung him severely. Calling to his son, who was sitting near him, he said, " My boy, there is a mosquito stinging my head, like the thrust of a spear— drive it off." "Wait a bit, father," said the boy, "and I will kill him with one blow." Then he took up an axe and stood behind his father's back ; and thinking to kill the mosquito with the axe, he only killed his father.

Among numerous variants is the story of the Sicilian booby, Giufà, who was annoyed by the flies, and complained of them to the judge, who told him that he was at liberty to kill a fly wherever he saw it: just then a fly happened to alight on the judge's nose, which Giufà observing, he immediately aimed at it so furious a blow with his fist, that he smashed his worship's nose!

The hopelessness of attempting to impart instruction to the silly son is farther illustrated by the story in a Sinhalese collection: A gûrû was engaged in teaching one of his disciples, but whilst he was teaching the youth was watching the movements of a rat which was entering its hole. As soon as the gûrû had finished his teaching, he said, " Well, my son, has all entered in ? " to which the youth replied, " Yes, all has entered in except the tail." And from the same work is the following choice example of " a happy family": A priest went one day to the house of one of his followers, and amongst other things he said, " Tell me now, which of your four children is the best-behaved ? " The father replied, " Look, sir, at that boy who has climbed to the top of that thatched building, and is waving aloft a firebrand. Among them all, he is the divinely excellent one." Whereupon the priest placed his finger on his nose, drew a deep, deep sigh, and said, "Is it indeed so? What, then, must the other three be?"

The Turkish romance of the Forty Vazírs —the plan of which is similar to that of the Book of Sindibád and its derivatives—furnishes us with two stories of the same class, one of which is as follows, according to my friend Mr. Gibb's complete translation (the first that has been made in English), recently published:[1]

They have told that in bygone times there was a king, and he had a skilful minstrel. One day a certain person gave to the latter a little boy, that he might teach him the science of music. The boy abode a long time by him, and though the master instructed him, he succeeded not in learning, and the master could make nothing of him. He arranged a scale, and said, "Whatsoever thou sayest to me, say in this scale." So whatsoever the boy said he used to say in that scale. Now one day a spark of fire fell on the master's turban. The boy saw it and chanted, "O master, I see something; shall I say it or no?" and he went over the whole scale. Then the master

[1] *History of the Forty Visiers; or, The Forty Morns and Forty Eves.* Translated from the Turkish, by E. J. W. Gibb, M.R.A.S. London: G. Redway, 1886.

chanted, " O boy, what dost thou see? Speak!" and he too went over all that the boy had gone over. Then the turn came to the boy, and he chanted, "O master, a spark has fallen on thy turban, and it is burning." The master straightway tore off his turban and cast it on the ground, and saw that it was burning. He blew out the fire on this side and on that, and took it in his hand, and said to the boy, " What time for chanting is this? Everything is good in its own place," and he admonished him. [1]

The other story tells how a king had a stupid son, and placed him in charge of a cunning master, learned in the sciences, who declared it would be easy for him to teach the boy discretion, and, before dismissing him, the king gave the sage many rich gifts. After the boy has been long under the tuition of his learned master, the latter, conceiving

[1] A variant of this is found in John Bromyard's *Summa Prædicantium*, A 26, 34, as follows:

Quidam sedebat juxta igneum, cujus vestem ignis intrabat. Dixit socius suus, "Vis audire rumores?" "Ita," inquit, "bonos et non alios." Cui alius, "Nescio nisi malos." "Ergo," inquit, "nolo audire." Et quum bis aut ter ei hoc diceret, semper idem respondit. In fine, quum sentiret vestem combustam, iratus ait socio, "Quare non dixisti mihi?" "Quia (inquit) dixista quod noluisti audire rumores nisi placentes et illi non erant tales."

him to be well versed in all the sciences, takes
him to the king, his father, who says to him,
"O my son, were I to hold a certain thing
hidden in my hand, couldst thou tell me what
it is?" "Yes," answers the youth. Upon
this the king secretly slips the ring off his
finger, and hides it in his hand, and then asks
the boy, "What have I in my hand?" Quoth
the clever youth, "O father, it first came from
the hills." (The king thinks to himself, "He
knows that mines are in the hills.") "And it
is a round thing," continues he—"it must be a
millstone." "Blockhead!" exclaims the irate
king, "could a millstone be hidden in a man's
hand?" Then addressing the learned man,
"Take him away," he says, "and *teach*
him."

Lastly, we have a somewhat different
specimen of the silly son in the doctor's
apprentice, whose attempt to imitate his
master was so ludicrously unsuccessful. He
used to accompany his master on his visits
to patients, and one day the doctor said to a
sick man, to whom he had been called, "I
know what is the matter with you, and it is
useless to deny it;—you have been eating
beans." On their way home, the apprentice,
admiring his master's sagacity, begged to be
informed how he knew that the patient had
been eating beans. "Boy," said the doctor,

loftily, "I drew an inference." "An inference!" echoed this youth of inquiring mind; "and what is an inference?" Quoth the doctor, "Listen: when we came to the door, I observed the shells of beans lying about, and I drew the inference that the family had had beans for dinner." Another day it chanced that the doctor did not take his apprentice with him when he went his rounds, and in his absence a message came for him to visit a person who had been taken suddenly ill. "Here," thought the apprentice, "is a chance for my putting master's last lesson into practice;" so off he went to the sick man, and assuming as "knowing" an air as he could, he felt his pulse, and then said to him severely, "Don't deny it; I see by your pulse that you have been eating a horse. I shall send you some medicine." When the doctor returned home he inquired of his hopeful pupil, whether any person had called for him, upon which the wittol proudly told him of his own exploit. "Eaten a horse!" exclaimed the man of physic. "In the name of all that's wonderful, what induced you to say such a thing?" Quoth the youth, simpering, "Why, sir, I did as you did the other day, when we visited the old farmer—I drew an inference." "You drew an inference, did you? And how did you draw the inference that the man had

eaten a horse?"   "Why, very readily, sir;
for as I entered the house I saw a saddle
hanging on the wall."[1]

[1] Under the title of "The Phisitian that bare
his Paciente in honde that he had eaten an Asse"
this jest occurs in *Merry Tales and Quicke Answeres*, and Professor Crane gives a Sicilian
version in hi *Italian Popular Tales.*

CHAPTER VI.

The Four Simple Bráhmans.

[As a sort of supplement to the sayings and doings of the silly son, the following highly diverting Indian tale is here inserted, from the Abbé Dubois' French rendering of the Tamil original, appended, with others, to his selections from the *Panchatantra.* The story is known in the north as well as in the south of India: in the Panjábi version there are, however, but three noodle-heroes. It will be seen that the third Bráhman's tale is another of the numerous silent couple class, and it may possibly be the original form.]

Introduction.

N a certain district, proclamation had been made of a Samaradanam being about to be held.[1] Four Bráhmans, from different villages going thither, fell in upon the road, and, finding that they were all upon the same errand, they agreed to proceed in company. A

[1] A Samaradanam is one of the public festivals given by pious people, and sometimes by those in power, to the Bráhmans, who on such occasions assemble in great numbers from all quarters.

soldier, happening to meet them, saluted
them in the usual way, by touching hands
and pronouncing the words always applied
on such occasions to Bráhmans, "*Dandamarya !*" or "Health to my lord !" The four
travellers made the customary return, "*Asirvadam !*" and going on, they came to a well,
where they quenched their thirst and reposed
themselves in the shade of some trees.
Sitting there, and finding no better subject of
conversation, one of them asked the others,
whether they did not remark how particularly the soldier had distinguished him by his
polite salutation. "You !" said another;
"it was not you that he saluted, but me."
"You are both mistaken," says a third; "for
you may remember that when the soldier
said, '*Dandamarya !*' he cast his eyes upon
me." "Not at all," replied the fourth; "it
was I only he saluted; otherwise, should I
have answered him as I did, by saying,
'*Asirvadam ?*"

Each maintained his argument obstinately;
and as none of them would yield, the dispute
had nearly come to blows, when the least
stupid of the four, seeing what was likely to
happen, put an end to the brawl by the
following advice : "How foolish it is in us,"
said he, "thus to put ourselves in a passion !
After we have said all the ill of one another

that we can invent—nay, after going stoutly to fisticuffs, like Sudra rabble, should we be at all nearer to the decision of our difference? The fittest person to determine the controversy, I think, would be the man who occasioned it. The soldier, who chose to salute one of us, cannot yet be far off: let us therefore run after him as quickly as we can, and we shall soon know for which of us he intended his salutation."

This advice appeared wise to them all, and was immediately adopted. The whole of them set off in pursuit of the soldier, and at last overtook him, after running a league, and all out of breath. As soon as they came in sight of him, they cried out to him to stop; and before they had well approached him, they had put him in full possession of the nature of their dispute, and prayed him to terminate it, by saying to which of them he had directed his salutation. The soldier instantly perceiving the character of the people he had to do with, and being willing to amuse himself a little at their expense, coolly replied, that he intended his salutation for the greatest fool of all four, and then, turning on his heel, he continued his journey.

The Bráhmans, confounded at this answer, turned back in silence. But all of them had deeply at heart the distinction of the salutation of the soldier, and the dispute was gradually renewed. Even the awkward decision of the warrior could not prevent each of them from arrogating to himself the pre-eminence of being noticed by him, to the exclusion of the others. The contention, therefore, now became, which of the four was the stupidest; and strange to say, it grew as warm as ever, and must have come to blows, had not the person who gave the former advice, to follow the soldier, interposed again with his wisdom, and spoken as follows : " I think myself the greatest fool of us all. Each of you thinks the same thing of himself. And after a fight, shall we be a bit nearer the decision of the question? Let us, therefore, have a little patience. We are within a short distance of Dharmapuri, where there is a choultry, at which all little causes are tried by the heads of the village; and let ours be judged among the rest."

The others agreed in the soundness of this advice; and having arrived at the village, they eagerly entered the choultry, to have their business settled by the arbitrator. They could not have come at a better season. The chiefs of the district, Bráhmans and others, had already met in the choultry; and no other cause being brought forward, they proceeded immediately to that of the four Bráhmans, who advanced into the middle of the court, and stated that a sharp contest having arisen among them, they were come to have it decided with fairness and impartiality. The court desired them to proceed and explain the ground of their controversy. Upon this, one of them stood forward and related to the assembly all that had happened, from their meeting with the soldier to the present state of the quarrel, which rested on the superior degree of stupidity of one of their number. The detail created a general shout of laughter. The president, who was of a gay disposition, was delighted beyond measure to have fallen in with so diverting an incident. But he put on a grave face, and laid it down, as the peculiarity of the cause, that it could not be determined on the testimony of witnesses, and that, in fact, there was no other way of satisfying the minds of the judges than by each, in his turn, relating some particular occurrence of his life, on which he could best establish his claim to superior folly. He clearly showed that there could be no other means of determining to which of them the salutation of the soldier could with justice be awarded. The Bráhmans assented, and upon a sign being made to one of them to begin, and the rest to keep silence, the first thus spoke :

Story of the First Bráhman.

I am poorly provided with clothing, as you
see ; and it is not to-day only that I have been
covered with rags. A rich and very charitable
Bráhman merchant once made a present of
two pieces of cloth to attire me—the finest
that had ever been seen in our village. I
showed them to the other Bráhmans of the
village, who all congratulated me on so fortunate an acquisition. They told me it must
be the fruit of some good deeds that I had
done in a preceding generation. Before I
should put them on, I washed them, according to the custom, in order to purify them
from the soil of the weaver's touch, and
hung them up to dry, with the ends fastened to two branches of a tree. A dog, then
happening to come that way, ran under them,
and I could not discover whether he was high
enough to touch the clothes or not. I asked
my children, who were present, but they said
they were not quite certain. How, then, was
I to discover the fact ? I put myself upon all-
fours, so as to be of the height of the dog,
and in that posture I crawled under the clothing. "Did I touch it ? " said I to the
children, who were observing me. They
answered, "No," and I was filled with joy
at the news. But after reflecting a while, I

recollected that the dog had a turned-up tail, and that by elevating it above the rest of his body, it might well have reached my cloth. To ascertain that, I fixed a leaf in my loin-cloth, turning upwards, and then, creeping again on all-fours, I passed a second time under the clothing. The children immediately cried out that the point of the leaf on my back had touched the cloth. This proved to me that the point of the dog's tail must have done so too, and that my garments were therefore polluted. In my rage I pulled down the beautiful raiment, and tore it in a thousand pieces, loading with curses both the dog and his master.

When this foolish act was known, I became the laughing-stock of all the world, and I was universally treated as a madman. " Even if the dog had touched the cloth," said they, "and so brought defilement upon it, might not you have washed it a second time, and so have removed the stain ? Or might you not have given it to some poor Sudra, rather than tear it in pieces ? After such egregious folly, who will give you clothes another time ? " This was all true ; for ever since, when I have begged clothing of any one, the constant answer has been, that, no doubt, I wanted a piece of cloth to pull to pieces.

He was going on, when a bystander inter-
rupted him by remarking that he seemed to
understand going on all-fours. " Exceedingly
well," said he, "as you shall see;" and off
he shuffled, in that posture, amidst the
unbounded   laughter   of   the   spectators.
"Enough! enough!" said the president.
" What we have both heard and seen goes
a great way in his favour. But let us now
hear what the next has to say for himself in
proof of his stupidity." The second accordingly began by expressing his confidence that
if what they had just heard appeared to them
to be deserving of the salutation of the
soldier, what he had to say would change
their opinion.

Story of the Second Bráhman.

Having got my hair and beard shaven one
day, in order to appear decent at a public
festival of the Bráhmans, which had been
proclaimed throughout the district, I desired
my wife to give the barber a penny for his
trouble. She heedlessly gave him a couple.
I asked him to give me one of them back,
but he refused. Upon that we quarrelled,
and began to abuse each other; but the
barber at length pacified me, by offering, in
consideration of the double fee, to shave
my wife also. I thought this a fair way of

settling the difference between us. But my wife, hearing the proposal, and seeing the barber in earnest, tried to make her escape by flight. I took hold of her, and forced her to sit down, while he shaved her poll in the same manner as they serve widows.[1] During the operation she cried out bitterly; but I was inexorable, thinking it less hard that my wife should be close-shaven than that my penny should be given away for nothing. When the barber had finished, I let her go, and she retired immediately to a place of concealment, pouring down curses on me and the barber. He took his departure, and meeting my mother in his way, told her what he had done, which made her hasten to the house, to inquire into the outrage; and when she saw that it was all true she also loaded me with incivilities.

The barber published everywhere what had happened at our house; and the villain added to the story that I had caught her with another man, which was the cause of

---

[1] In a Sinhalese story, referred to on p. 68, it is, curiously enough, the woman herself "who has her head shaved, so as not to lose the services of the barber for the day when he came, and her husband was away from home." The story probably was introduced into Ceylon by the Tamils; both versions are equally good as noodle-stories.

my having her shaved; and people were no doubt expecting, according to our custom in such a case, to see her mounted on an ass, with her face turned towards the tail. They came running to my dwelling from all quarters, and actually brought an ass to make the usual exhibition in the streets. The report soon reached my father-in-law, who lived at a distance of ten or twelve leagues, and he, with his wife, came also to inquire into the affair. Seeing their poor daughter in that degraded state, and being apprised of the only reason, they reproached me most bitterly; which I patiently endured, being conscious that I was in the wrong. They persisted, however, in taking her with them, and keeping her carefully concealed from every eye for four whole years; when at length they restored her to me.

This little accident made me lose the Samaradanam, for which I had been preparing by a fast of three days; and it was a great mortification to me to be excluded from it, as I understood it was a most splendid entertainment. Another Samaradanam was announced to be held ten days afterwards, at which I expected to make up for my loss. But I was received with the hisses of six hundred Bráhmans, who seized my person, and insisted on my giving up the accomplice of my wife, that he might be prosecuted and punished, according to the severe rules of the caste.

I solemnly attested her innocence, and told the real cause of the shaving of her hair; when a universal burst of surprise took place, every one exclaiming, how monstrous it was that a married woman should be so degraded, without having committed the crime of infidelity. "Either this man," said they, "must be a liar, or he is the greatest fool on the face of the earth!" Such, I daresay, gentlemen, you will think me, and I am sure you will consider my folly [looking with great disdain on the first speaker] as being far superior to that of the render of body-clothing.

The court agreed that the speaker had put in a very strong case; but justice required that the other two should also be heard.[1] The third claimant was indeed burning with impatience for his turn, and as soon as he had permission, he thus spoke:

Story of the Third Bráhman.

My name was originally Anantya; now all the world call me Betel Anantya, and I will tell you how this nickname arose. My wife, having been long detained at her father's house, on account of her youth, had cohabited with me but about a month when, going to bed one evening, I happened to say (carelessly, I believe), that all women were babblers. She retorted, that she knew men who were not less babblers than women. I perceived at once that she alluded to myself; and being somewhat piqued at the sharpness of her retort, I said, " Now let us see which of us shall speak first." "Agreed," quoth she; " but what shall be the forfeit ? " "A leaf of betel," said I. Our wager being thus made, we both addressed ourselves to sleep, without speaking another word.

Next morning, as we did not appear at our usual hour, after some interval, they called us, but got no answer. They again called, and then roared stoutly at the door, but with no success. The alarm began to spread in the house. They began to fear that we had died suddenly. The carpenter was called with his tools. The door of our room was forced open, and when they got in they were not a little surprised to find both of us wide awake, in good health, and at our ease, though without the faculty of speech. My mother was greatly alarmed, and gave loud vent to her grief. All the Bráhmans in the village, of both sexes, assembled, to the number of one hundred; and after close examination, every one drew his own conclusion on the accident

which was supposed to have befallen us.
The greater number were of opinion that it
could have arisen only from the malevolence
of some enemy who had availed h'mself of
magical incantations to injure us. For this
reason, a famous magician was called, to
counteract the effects of the witchcraft, and to
remove it. As soon as he came, after steadfastly contemplating us for some time, he
began to try our pulses, by putting his finger
on our wrists, on our temples, on the heart,
and on various other parts of the body; and
after a great variety of grimaces, the remem-
brance of which excites my laughter, as often
as I think of him, he decided that our malady
arose wholly from the effect of malevolence.
He even gave the name of the particular devil
that possessed my wife and me and rendered
us dumb. He added that the devil was very
stubborn and difficult to allay, and that it
would cost three or four pagodas for the
offerings necessary for compelling him to
fly.

My relations, who were not very opulent,
were astonished at the grievous imposition
which the magician had laid on them. Yet,
rather than we should continue dumb, they
consented to give him whatsoever should be
necessary for the expense of his sacrifice ; and
they farther promised that they would reward

him for his trouble as soon as the demon by
whom we were possessed should be expelled.
He was on the point of commencing his
magical operations, when a Bráhman, one of
our friends, who was present, maintained, in
opposition to the opinion of the magician and
his assistants, that our malady was not at
all the effect of witchcraft, but arose from
some simple and ordinary cause, of which he
had seen several instances, and he undertook
to cure us without any expense.

He took a chafing-dish filled with burning
charcoal, and heated a small bar of gold very
hot. This he took up with pincers, and applied to the soles of my feet, then to my
elbows, and the crown of my head. I endured these cruel operations without showing
the least symptom of pain, or making any
complaint; being determined to bear anything, and to die, if necessary, rather than
lose the wager I had laid.

"Let us try the effect on the woman," said
the doctor, astonished at my resolution and
apparent insensibility. And immediately
taking the bit of gold, well heated, he applied it to the sole of her foot. She was not
able to endure the pain for a moment, but
instantly screamed out, "Enough!" and turning to me, "I have lost my wager," she said;
"there is your leaf of betel." "Did I not

tell you," said I, taking the leaf, "that you would be the first to speak out, and that you would prove by your own conduct that I was right in saying yesterday, when we went to bed, that women are babblers ? "

Every one was surprised at the proceeding; nor could any of them comprehend the meaning of what was passing between my wife and me ; until I explained the kind of wager we had made overnight, before going to sleep. " What ! " they exclaimed, " was it for a leaf of betel that you have spread this alarm through your own house and the whole village ?—for a leaf of betel that you showed such constancy, and suffered burning from the feet to the head upwards ?   Never in the world was there seen such folly ! " And so, from that time, I have been constantly known by the name of Betel Anantya.

The narrative being finished, the court were of opinion that so transcendent a piece of folly gave him high pretensions in the depending suit ; but it was necessary also to hear the fourth and last of the suitors, who thus addressed them :

Story of the Fourth Bráhman.

The maiden to whom I was betrothed, having remained six or seven years at her father's

house, on account of her youth, we were at
last apprised that she was become marriage-
able; and her parents informed mine that she
was in a situation to fulfil all the duties of a
wife, and might therefore join her husband.
My mother being at that time sick, and the
house of my father-in-law being at the distance of five or six leagues from ours, she
was not able to undertake the journey.   She
therefore committed to myself the duty of
bringing home my wife, and counselled me
so to conduct myself, in words and actions,
that they might not see that I was only a
brute. "Knowing thee as I do," said my
mother, as I took leave of her, "I am very
distrustful of thee."   But I promised to be on
my good behaviour; and so I departed.

   I was well received by my father-in-law,
who gave a great feast to all the Bráhmans of
the village on the occasion. He made me
stay three days, during which there was
nothing but festivity. At length the time of
our departure having arrived, he suffered my
wife and myself to leave him, after pouring
out blessings on us both, and wishing us a
long and happy life, enriched with a numerous progeny. When we took leave of him,
he shed abundance of tears, as if he had fore-
seen the misery that awaited us.

   It was then the summer solstice, and the

day was exceedingly hot. We had to cross a sandy plain of more than two leagues ; and the sand, being heated by the burning sun, scorched the feet of my young wife, who, being brought up too tenderly in her father's house, was not accustomed to such severe trials. She began to cry, and being unable to go on, she lay down on the ground, saying she wished to die there. I was in dreadful trouble, and knew not what step to take ; when a merchant came up, travelling the contrary way. He had a train of fifty bullocks, loaded with various kinds of merchandise. I ran to meet him, and told him the cause of my anxiety with tears in my eyes; and entreated him to aid me with his good advice in the distressing circumstances in which I was placed. He immediately answered, that a young and delicate woman, such as my wife was, could neither remain where she lay nor proceed on her journey, under a hot sun, without being exposed to certain death. Rather than that I should see her perish, and run the hazard of being suspected of having killed her myself, and being guilty of one of the five crimes which the Bráhmans consider as the most heinous, he advised me to give her to him, and then he would mount her on one of his cattle and take her along with him. That I should be a loser, he admitted ; but, all things considered, it was better to lose her, with the merit of having saved her life, than equally to lose her, under the suspicion of being her murderer. " Her trinkets," he said, " may be worth fifteen pagodas ; take these twenty and give me your wife."

The merchant's arguments appeared unanswerable; so I yielded to them, and delivered to him my wife, whom he placed on one of his best oxen, and continued his journey without delay. I continued mine also, and got home in the evening, exhausted with hunger and fatigue, and with my feet almost roasted with the burning sand, over which I had walked the greater part of the day. Frightened to see me alone, "Where is your wife?" cried my mother. I gave her a full account of everything that had happened from the time I left her. I spoke of the agreeable and courteous manner in which my father-in-law had received me, and how, by some delay, we had been overtaken by the scorching heat of the sun at noon, so that my wife must have perished and myself suspected of having caused her death, had we proceeded; and that I had preferred to sell her to a merchant who met us for twenty pagodas. And I showed my mother the money.

When I had done, my mother fell into an

ecstasy ot fury. She lifted up her voice against me with cries of rage, and over-whelmed me with imprecations and awful curses. Having given way to these first emotions of despair, she sank into a more moderate tone: "What hast thou done! Sold thy wife, hast thou! Delivered her to another man! A Bráhmanari is become the concubine of a vile merchant! Ah, what will her kindred and ours say when they hear the tale of this brutish stupidity—of folly so unexampled and degrading?"

The relations of my wife were soon in-formed of the sad adventure that had befallen their unhappy girl. They came over to attack me, and would certainly have murdered me and my innocent mother, if we had not both made a sudden escape. Having no direct object to wreak their vengeance upon, they brought the matter before the chiefs of the caste, who unanimously fined me in two hundred pagodas, as a reparation to my father-in-law, and issued a proclamation against so great a fool being ever allowed to take another wife; denouncing the penalty of expulsion from the caste against any one who should assist me in such an attempt. I was there-fore condemned to remain a widower all my life, and to pay dear for my folly. Indeed, I should have been excluded for ever from my caste, but for the high consideration in which the memory of my late father is still held, he having lived respected by all the world.

Now that you have heard one specimen ot the many follies of my life, I hope you will not consider me as beneath those who have spoken before me, nor my pretensions altogether undeserving of the salutation of the soldier.

Conclusion.

The heads of the assembly, several of whom were convulsed with laughter while the Bráhmans were telling their stories, decided, after hearing them all, that each had given such absolute proofs of folly as to be entitled, in justice, to a superiority in his own way: that each of them, therefore, should be at liberty to call himself the greatest fool of all, and to attribute to himself the salutation of the soldier. Each of them having thus gained his suit, it was recommended to them all to continue their journey, if it were possible, in amity. The delighted Bráhmans then rushed out of court, each exclaiming that he had gained his cause.

CHAPTER VII.

THE THREE GREAT NOODLES.

EW folk-tales are more widely diffused than that of the man who set out in quest of as great noodles as those of his own household. The details may be varied more or less, but the fundamental outline is identical, wherever the story is found; and, whether it be an instance of the transmission of popular tales from one country to another, or one of those " primitive fictions " which are said to be the common heritage of the Aryans, its independent development by different nations and in different ages cannot be reasonably maintained.

Thus, in one Gaelic version of this diverting story—in which our old friends the Gothamites reappear on the scene to enact their unconscious drolleries—a lad marries a farmer's daughter, and one day while they are all busily engaged in peat-cutting, she is sent

to the house to fetch the dinner. On entering the house, she perceives the speckled
pony's packsaddle hanging from the roof, and
says to herself, "Oh, if that packsaddle were
to fall and kill me, what should I do?" and
here she began to cry, until her mother, won-
dering what could be detaining her, comes,
when she tells the old woman the cause of
her grief, whereupon the mother, in her turn,
begins to cry, and when the old man next
comes to see what is the matter with his wife
and daughter, and is informed about the
speckled pony's packsaddle, he, too, "mingles
his tears" with theirs. At last the young
husband arrives, and finding the trio of
noodles thus grieving at an imaginary misfortune, he there and then leaves them, declaring his purpose not to return until he has
found three as great fools as themselves. In
the course of his travels he meets with some
strange folks: men whose wives make them
believe whatever they please—one, that he is
dead; another, that he is clothed, when he is
stark naked; a third, that he is not himself.
He meets with the twelve fishers who always
miscounted their number; the noodles who
went to drown an eel in the sea; and a man
trying to get his cow on the roof of his house,
in order that she might eat the grass growing
there. But the most wonderful incident was

a man coming with a cow in a cart: and the people had found out that the man had stolen the cow, and that a court should be held upon him, and so they did; and the justice they did was to put the horse to death for carrying the cow.[1]

In another Gaelic version a young husband had provided his house with a cradle, in natural anticipation that such an interesting piece of furniture would be required in due time. In this he was disappointed, but the cradle stood in the kitchen all the same. One day he chanced to throw something into the empty cradle, upon which his wife, his mother, and his wife's mother set up loud lamentations, exclaiming, "Oh, if *he* had been there, he had been killed!" alluding to a potential son. The man was so much shocked at such an exhibition of folly that he left the country in search of three greater noodles. Among other adventures, he goes into a house and plays tricks on some people there, telling

[1] Campbell's *Popular Tales of the West Highlands*, vol. ii., pp. 373—381. In a note to these adventures Campbell gives a story of some women who, as judges, doomed a horse to be hanged: the thief who stole the horse got off, because it was his first offence; the horse went back to the house of the thief, because he was the better master, and was condemned for stealing himself!

13

them his name is "*Saw ye ever my like?*"
When the old man of the house comes home
he finds his people tied upon tables, and asks,
"What's the reason of this?" "Saw ye ever
my like?" says the first. Then going to a
second man, he asks, "What's the reason of
this?" "Saw ye ever my like?" says the
second. "I saw thy like in the kitchen,"
replies the old man, and then he goes to the
third: "What's the reason of this?" "Saw
ye ever my like?" says the third. "I have
seen plenty of thy like," quoth the old man;
"but never before this day," and then he
understood that some one had been playing
tricks on his people.[1]

[1] Campbell's *Popular Tales of the West Highlands*, vol. ii., pp. 385—387.
In a Northumberland popular tale a child in
bed sees a little fairy come down the chimney,
and the child tells the creature that his name is
My-ainsel. They play together, and the little
fairy is burnt with a cinder, and on its mother
appearing when it cries, and asking it who had
hurt it, the imp answers, "It was My-ainsel."—
There is a somewhat similar story current in
Finland: A man is moulding lead buttons, when
the Devil appears, and asks him what he is
doing. "Making eyes." "Could you make me
new ones?" "Yes." So he ties the Devil to a
bench, and, in reply to the fiend, tells him that
his name is Myself (*Issi*), and then pours lead
into his eyes. The Devil starts up with the
bench on his back, and runs off howling. Some

In Russian variants the old parents of a youth named Lutonya weep over the supposititious death of a potential grandchild, thinking how sad it would have been if a log which the old woman had dropped had killed that hypothetical infant. The parents' grief appears to Lutonya so uncalled for that he leaves the house, declaring he will not return until he has met with people more foolish than they. He travels long and far, and sees several foolish doings. In one place a horse is being inserted into its collar by sheer force; in another, a woman is fetching milk from the cellar a spoonful at a time; and in a third place some carpenters are attempting to stretch a beam which is not long enough, and Lutonya earns their gratitude by showing them how to join a piece to it.[1]

people working in a field ask him who did it Quoth the fiend, "Myself did it" (*Issi teggi*).

Cf. the *Odyssey*, Book ix., where Ulysses informs the Cyclops that his name is No-man, and when the monster, after having had his eye put out in his sleep, awakes in agony, he roars to his comrades for help:

" Friends, No-man kills me, No-man, in the hour
Of sleep, oppresses me with fraudful power ! "
" If no man hurt thee, but the hand divine
Inflict disease, it fits thee to resign ;—
To Jove, or to thy father, Neptune, pray,"
The brethren cried, and instant strode away.

---

[1] Ralston's *Russian Folk-Tales.*

A well-known English version is to this
effect: There was a young man who courted
a farmer's daughter, and one evening when
he came to the house she was sent to the
cellar for beer. Seeing an axe stuck in a
beam above her head, she thought to herself,
"Suppose I were married and had a son, and
he were to grow up, and be sent to this cellar
for beer, and this axe were to fall and kill
him—oh dear! oh dear!" and there she sat
crying and crying, while the beer flowed all
over the cellar-floor, until her old father and
mother come in succession and blubber along
with her about the hypothetical death of her
imaginary grown-up son. The young man
goes off in quest of three bigger fools, and
sees a woman hoisting a cow on to the roof
of her cottage to eat the grass that grew
among the thatch, and to keep the animal
from falling off, she ties a rope round its
neck, then goes into the kitchen, secures at
her waist the rope, which she had dropped
down the chimney, and presently the cow
stumbles over the roof, and the woman is
pulled up the flue till she sticks half-way.
In an inn he sees a man attempting to jump
into his trousers—a favourite incident in this
class of stories; and farther along he meets
with a party raking the moon out of a pond.

Another English variant relates that a young

girl having been left alone in the house, her mother finds her in tears when she comes home, and asks the cause of her distress. "Oh," says the girl, "while you were away, a brick fell down the chimney, and I thought, if it had fallen on me I might have been killed!" The only novel adventure which the girl's betrothed meets with, in his quest of three bigger fools, is an old woman trying to drag an oven with a rope to the table where the dough lay.

Several versions are current in Italy and Sicily, which present a close analogy to those of other European countries. The following is a translation of one in Bernoni's Venetian collection:

Once upon a time there were a husband and a wife who had a son. This son grew up, and said one day to his mother, "Do you know, mother, I would like to marry?" "Very well, marry! Whom do you want to take?" He answered, "I want the gardener's daughter." "She is a good girl—take her; I am willing." So he went, and asked for the girl, and her parents gave her to him. They were married, and when they were in the midst of their dinner, the wine gave out. The husband said, "There is no more wine!" The bride, to show that she was a good

housekeeper, said, "I will go and get some."
She took the bottles and went to the cellar,
turned the cock, and began to think, "Suppose
I should have a son, and we should call him
Bastianelo, and he should die! Oh, how
grieved I should be! oh, how grieved I should
be!" And thereupon she began to weep and
weep; and meanwhile the wine was running
all over the cellar.

When they saw that the bride did not
return, the mother said, "I will go and see
what the matter is." So she went into the
cellar, and saw the bride, with the bottle in
her hand, and weeping. "What is the
matter with you that you are weeping?"
"Ah, my mother, I was thinking that if I
had a son, and should name him Bastianelo,
and he should die, oh, how I should grieve!
oh, how I should grieve!" The mother, too,
began to weep, and weep, and weep; and
meanwhile the wine was running over the
cellar.

When the people at the table saw that no
one brought the wine, the groom's father
said, "I will go and see what is the matter.
Certainly something wrong has happened to
the bride." He went and saw the whole
cellar full of wine, and the mother and bride
weeping. "What is the matter?" he said;
"has anything wrong happened to you?"

'No," said the bride; "but I was thinking that if I had a son, and should call him Bastianelo, and he should die, oh, how I should grieve! oh, how I should grieve!" Then he, too, began to weep, and all three wept; and meanwhile the wine was running over the cellar.

When the groom saw that neither the bride, nor the mother, nor the father came back, he said, "Now I will go and see what the matter is that no one returns." He went into the cellar and saw all the wine running over the cellar. He hastened and stopped the cask, and then asked, "What is the matter that you are all weeping, and have let the wine run all over the cellar?" Then the bride said, "I was thinking that if I had a son and called him Bastianelo, and he should die, oh, how I should grieve! oh, how I should grieve!" Then the groom said, "You stupid fools! Are you weeping at this and letting all the wine run into the cellar? Have you nothing else to think of? It shall never be said that I remained with you. I will roam about the world, and until I find three fools greater than you, I will not return home."

He had a bread-cake made, took a bottle of wine, a sausage, and some linen, and made a bundle, which he put on a stick and carried over his shoulder. He journeyed and journeyed, but found no fool. At last he said, worn out, "I must turn back, for I see I cannot find a greater fool than my wife." He did not know what to do, whether to go on or turn back. "Oh," said he, "it is better to try and go a little farther." So he went on, and shortly saw a man in his shirt-sleeves at a well, all wet with perspiration, and water. "What are you doing, sir, that you are so covered with water and in such a sweat?" "Oh, let me alone," the man answered; "for I have been here a long time drawing water to fill this pail, and I cannot fill it." "What are you drawing the water in?" he asked him. "In this sieve," he said. "What are you thinking about, to draw water in that sieve? Just wait!" He went to a house near by and borrowed a bucket, with which he returned to the well and filled the pail. "Thank you, good man. God knows how long I should have had to remain here!"—"Here," thought he, "is one who is a greater fool than my wife."

He continued his journey, and after a time he saw at a distance a man in his shirt, who was jumping down from a tree. He drew near, and saw a woman under the same tree, holding a pair of breeches. He asked them what they were doing, and they said

that they had been there a long time, and
that the man was trying on those breeches
and did not know how to get into them. "I
have jumped and jumped," said the man,
"until I am tired out, and I cannot imagine
how to get into those breeches." "Oh," said
the traveller, "you might stay here as long as
you wished, for you would never get into them
this way. Come down and lean against the
tree." Then he took his legs and put them
in the breeches, and after he had put them
on, he said, "Is that right?" "Very
good; bless you; for if it had not been for
you, God knows how long I should have
had to jump." Then the traveller said to
himself, "I have seen two greater fools than
my wife."

Then he went his way, and as he approached
a city, he heard a great noise. When he
drew near he asked what it was, and was
told it was a marriage, and that it was the
custom in that city for the brides to enter
the city gate on horseback, and that there
was a great discussion on this occasion between the groom and the owner of the horse,
for the bride was tall and the horse high, and
they could not get through the gate; so that
they must either cut off the bride's head or
the horse's legs. The groom did not wish
his bride's head cut off, and the owner of the

horse did not wish his horse's legs cut off, and hence this disturbance. Then the traveller said, "Just wait," and came up to the bride and gave her a slap that made her lower her head, and then he gave the horse a kick, and so they passed through the gate and entered the city. The groom and the owner of the horse asked the traveller what he wanted, for he had saved the groom his bride and the owner of the horse his horse. He answered that he did not wish anything, and said to himself, "Two and one make three! that is enough. Now I will go home." He did so, and said to his wife, "Here I am, my wife; I have seen three greater fools than you ;—now let us remain in peace, and think of nothing else." They renewed the wedding, and always remained in peace. After a time the wife had a son, whom they named Bastianelo, and Bastianelo did not die, but still lives with his father and mother.[1]

There is (Professor Crane remarks) a Sicilian version in Pitré's collection, called "The Peasant of Larcàra," in which the bride's mother imagines that her daughter has a son who falls into the cistern. The groom

---

[1] Crane's *Italian Popular Tales*, pp. 279—282.

—they are not yet married—is disgusted, and sets out on his travels with no fixed purpose of returning if he finds some fools greater than his mother-in-law, as in the Venetian tale. The first fool he meets is a mother, whose child, in playing the game called *nocciole*,[1] tries to get his hand out of the hole whilst his fist is full of stones. He cannot, of course, and the mother thinks they will have to cut off his hand. The traveller tells the child to drop the stones, and then he draws out his hand easily enough. Next he finds a bride who cannot enter the church because she is very tall and wears a high comb. The difficulty is settled as in the former story. After a while he comes to a woman who is spinning and drops her spindle. She calls out to the pig, whose name is Tony, to pick it up for her. The pig does nothing but grunt, and the woman in anger cries, "Well, you won't pick it up? May your mother die!" The traveller, who had overheard all this, takes a piece of paper, which he folds up like a letter, and then knocks at the door. "Who is there?" "Open the door, for I have a letter for you from Tony's mother, who is ill and wishes

---

[1] A game played with peach-pits, which are thrown into holes made in the ground, and to which certain numbers are attached.

to see her son before she dies." The woman
wonders that her imprecation has taken effect
so soon, and readily consents to Tony's
visit. Not only this, but she loads a mule
with everything necessary for the comfort of
the body and soul of the dying pig. The
traveller leads away the mule with Tony,
and returns home so pleased with having
found that the outside world contains so
many fools that he marries as he had first
intended.[1]

In other Italian versions, a man is trying
to jump into his stockings; another endea-
vours to put walnuts into a sack with a fork;
and a woman dips a knotted rope into a deep
well, and then having drawn it up, squeezes
the water out of the knots into a pail. The
final adventure of the traveller in quest of the
greatest noodles is thus related in Miss
Busk's *Folk-lore of Rome :*

Towards nightfall he arrived at a lone
cottage, where he knocked, and asked for
a night's lodging. "I can't give you that,"
said a voice from the inside; "for I am a
lone widow. I can't take a man in to sleep
here." "But I am a pilgrim," replied he;
"let me in at least to cook a bit of supper."

---

[1] Crane's *Italian Popular Tales*, pp. 282-3.

"That I don't mind doing," said the good wife, and she opened the door. "Thanks, good friend," said the pilgrim, as he sat down by the stove. "Now add to your charity a couple of eggs in a pan." So she gave him a pan and two eggs, and a bit of butter to cook them in ; but he took the six eggs out of his staff and broke them into the pan too. Presently, when the good wife turned her head his way again, and saw eight eggs swimming in the pan instead of two, she said, "Lack-a-day! you must surely be some strange being from the other world. Do you know So-and-so ?" naming her husband. "Oh yes," said he, enjoying the joke; "I know him very well: he lives just next to me." "Only to think of that!" replied the poor woman. "And, do tell me, how do you get on in the other world? What sort of a life is it?" "Oh, not so very bad; it depends what sort of a place you get. The part where we are is pretty good, except that we get very little to eat. Your husband, for instance, is nearly starved." "No, really?" cried the good wife, clasping her hands. "Only fancy, my good husband starving out there, so fond as he was of a good dinner, too!" Then she added, coaxingly, "As you know him so well, perhaps you wouldn't mind doing him the charity of taking him a little somewhat, to give him a treat. There are such lots of things I could easily send him." "Oh dear, no, not at all. I'll do so with pleasure," answered he. "But I'm not going back till to-morrow, and if I don't sleep here I must go on farther, and then I shan't come by this way." "That's true," replied the widow. "Ah, well, I mustn't mind what the folks say; for such an opportunity as this may never occur again. You must sleep in my bed, and I must sleep on the hearth ; and in the morning I'll load a donkey with provisions for my poor husband." "Oh, no," replied the pilgrim, "you shan't be disturbed in your bed. Only let me sleep on the hearth—that will do for me ; and as I am an early riser, I can be gone before any one's astir, so folks won't have anything to say."

So it was done, and an hour before sunrise the woman was up, loading the donkey with the best of her stores—ham, macaroni, flour, cheese, and wine. All this she committed to the pilgrim, saying, "You'll send the donkey back, won't you?" "Of course I would send him back," he replied ; "he'd be of no use to me out there. But I shan't get out again myself for another hundred years or so, and I fear he won't find his way back alone, for it's no easy way to find." "To be sure not ; I ought to have thought of that," replied

the widow. "Ah, well, so as my poor husband gets a good meal, never mind the
donkey." So the pretended pilgrim from the
other world went his way. He hadn't gone a
hundred yards before the widow called him
back. "Ah, she's beginning to think better
of it," said he to himself, and he continued
his way, pretending not to hear. "Good pilgrim," shouted the widow, "I forgot one
thing: would money be of any use to my
poor husband?" "Oh dear, yes," said he,
"all the use in the world. You can always
get anything for money anywhere." "Oh, do
come back, then, and I'll trouble you with
a hundred scudi for him." He went back,
willingly, for the hundred scudi, which the
widow counted out to him. "There's no
help for it," said he to himself as he went
his way: "I must go back to those at
home."

From sunny Italy to bleak Norway is
certainly a "far cry," yet the adventure of
the "Pilgrim from Paradise" is also known
to the Norse peasants, in connection with the
quest of the greatest noodles: A goody goes
to market, with a cow and a hen for sale.
She wants five shillings for the cow and ten
pounds for the hen. A butcher buys the
cow, but doesn't want the hen. As she can-

not find a buyer for the hen, she goes back
to the butcher, who treats her to so much
brandy that she gets dead-drunk, and in this
condition the butcher tars and feathers her.
When she awakes, she fancies that she must
be some strange bird, and cries out, "Is this
me, or is it not me? I'll go home, and if our
dog barks, then it is not me." Thus far we have
a variant of our favourite nursery rhyme:

There was an old woman, as I've heard tell,
She went to market her eggs for to sell;
She went to market, all on a market-day,
And she fell asleep on the king's highway.

There came a pedlar, whose name was Stout,
He cut her petticoats all round about;
He cut her petticoats up to the knees,
Which made the old woman to shiver and
        freeze.

When the little woman first did wake,
She began to shiver and she began to shake;
She began to wonder, and she began to cry,
"Lauk-a-mercy on me, this is none of I!"

"But if this be I, as I do hope it be,
I've a little dog at home, and he'll know me;
If it be I, he'll wag his little tail,
And if it be not I, he loudly bark and wail."

Home went the little woman all in the dark,
Up got the little dog, and began to bark;
He began to bark, and she began to cry,
"Lauk-a-mercy on me, this can't be I!"

To return to the Norse tale. As in our nursery rhyme, when the goody reaches home, the dog barks at her; then she goes to the calves' house, but the calves, having sniffed the tar with which she was smeared, turn away from her in disgust. She is now fully convinced that she has been transformed into some outlandish bird, so she climbs on to the roof of a shed, and begins to flap her arms as if she were about to fly, when out comes her goodman, and seeing a suspicious-looking creature on the roof of the shed, he fetches his gun and is going to shoot at his goody, when he recognises her voice. Amazed at such a piece of folly, he resolves to leave her and not come back till he has found three goodies as silly. He meets with a female descendant of the Schildburgers, evidently, carrying into her cottage sunshine in a sieve, there being no window in the house: he cuts out a window for her and is well paid for his trouble. He next comes to a house where an old woman is thumping her goodman on the head with a beetle, in order to force over him a shirt without a slit for the neck, which she had drawn over his head: he cuts a slit in the shirt with a pair of scissors, and is amply rewarded for his ingenuity. His third adventure is similar to that of the "pilgrim" in the Italian version :

14

At another house he informs the goody that he came from Paradise Place—which was the name of his own farm—and she asks him if he knew her second husband in paradise. (She had been married twice before she took her present husband, who was an old curmudgeon, and she liked her second husband best—she was sure he had gone to heaven.) He replies that he knew him very intimately, but, poor man, he was far from well off, having to go about begging from house to house. The goody gives him a cart-load of clothes and a box of shining dollars, for her dear second husband; for why should he go about begging in paradise when there was so much of everything in their house? So the stranger jumps into the cart and drives off, as fast as possible. But Peter, the goody's third husband, sees him on the road, and recognising his own horse and cart, hastens home to his wife, and asks why a stranger has gone off with his property. She explains the whole affair, upon which he mounts a horse and gallops away after the rogue who had thus taken advantage of his wife's simplicity. The stranger, perceiving him approach, hides the horse and cart behind a high hedge, takes part of the horse's tail and hangs it on the branches of a birch-tree, and then lays himself down on his back and gazes up into the sky. When Peter comes up to him, he exclaims, still looking at the sky, "What a wonder there is a man going straight to heaven on a black horse!" Peter can see no such thing. "Can you not?" says the stranger. "See, there is his tail, still on the birch-tree. You must lie down in this very spot, and look straight up, and don't for a moment take your eyes off the sky, and then you'll see—what you'll see." So Peter lies down and gazes up at the sky very intently, looking for the man going straight to heaven on a black horse. Meanwhile the traveller escapes, with the cart-load of clothes and the box of shining dollars, and the second horse besides. Peter, when he reaches home, tells his wife that he had given the man from paradise the other horse for her second husband to ride about on, for he was ashamed to confess that he had been cheated as well as herself.[1] As to our traveller, having found three goodies as great fools as his own, he returned home, and saw that all his fields had been ploughed and sown ; so he asked his wife where she had got the seed from. "Oh," says she, "I have always heard that what a man sows he shall also reap, so I sowed the salt that our friends the north-countrymen laid up with us, and if we

[1] The same story is told in Brittany, with no important variations.

only have rain, I fancy it will come up nicely."[1]
"Silly you are," said her husband, "and silly
you will be as long as you live.   But that is
all one now, for the rest are not a bit wiser
than you ;—*there is not a pin to choose between
you !*"[2]

Now, if it be "a far cry" from Italy to
Norway, it is still farther from Norway to
India ; and yet it is in the southern provinces
of our great Asiatic empire that a story is
current among the people, which, strange as
it may seem, is almost the exact counterpart
of the Norse version of the pretended pilgrim
from paradise, of which the above is an
abstract.   It is found in Pandit S. M. Natésa
Sástrí's *Folk-lore in Southern India*, now in
course of publication at Bombay ; a work
which, when completed, will be of very great
value to students of comparative folk-tales,

[1] Quite as literally did the rustic understand
the priest's assurance, that whatsoever one gave
in charity, for the love of God, should be repaid
him twofold : next day he takes his cow to the
priest, who accepts it as sent by Heaven—and the
poor man did *not* get two cows in return.   The
story is known in various forms all over Europe ;
it was a special favourite in mediæval times.
See Le Grand's *Fabliaux*, tome iii., 376: "La
Vache du Curé," by the trouvère Jean de Boves ;
Wright's *Latin Stories ; Icelandic Legends*, etc.
    Dasent's *Popular Tales from the Norse.*

as well as prove an entertaining story-book for general readers. After condensation in some parts, this story—which the Pandit entitles " The Good Wife and the Bad Husband "— runs thus :

In a secluded village there lived a rich man, who was very miserly, and his wife, who was very kind-hearted and charitable, but a stupid little woman that believed everything shé heard. And there lived in the same village a clever rogue, who had for some time watched for an opportunity for getting something from this simple woman during her husband's absence. So one day, when he had seen the old miser ride out to inspect his lands, this rogue of the first water came to the house, and fell down at the threshold as if overcome by fatigue. The woman ran up to him at once and inquired whence he came. "I am come from Kailása,"[1] said he ; "having been sent down by an old couple living there, for news of their son and his wife." "Who are those fortunate dwellers in Siva's mountain ? " she asked. And the rogue gave the names of her husband's deceased parents, which he had taken good care, of course, to learn from the neighbours. "Do you really come from them ? " said the simple woman. "Are they doing well there ? Dear old people ! How glad

[1] See note, p. 49.

my husband would be to see you, were he
here! Sit down, please, and rest until he
returns. How do they live there? Have they
enough to eat and dress themselves withal?"
These and a hundred other questions she put
to the rogue, who, for his part, wished to get
away as soon as possible, knowing full well
how he would be treated if the miser should
return while he was there. So he replied,
"Mother, language has no words to describe
the miseries they are undergoing in the other
world. They have not a rag of clothing, and
for the last six days they have eaten nothing,
and have lived on water only. It would break
your heart to see them." The rogue's
pathetic words deceived the good woman,
who firmly believed that he had come down
from Kailása, a messenger from the old couple
to herself. "Why should they so suffer,"
said she, "when their son has plenty to eat
and clothe himself withal, and when their
daughter-in-law wears all sorts of costly
garments?" So saying, she went into the
house, and soon came out again with two
boxes containing all her own and her husband's clothes, which she handed to the rogue,
desiring him to deliver them to the poor old
couple in Kailása. She also gave him her
jewel-box, to be presented to her mother-in-
law. "But dress and jewels will not fill their

hungry stomachs," said the rogue. "Very true; I had forgot: wait a moment," said the simple woman, going into the house once more. Presently returning with her husband's cash chest, she emptied its glittering contents into the rogue's skirt, who now took his leave in haste, promising to give everything to the good old couple in Kailása; and having secured all the booty in his upper garment, he made off at the top of his speed as soon as the silly woman had gone indoors.

Shortly after this the husband returned home, and his wife's pleasure at what she had done was so great that she ran to meet him at the door, and told him all about the arrival of the messenger from Kailása, how his parents were without clothes and food, and how she had sent them clothes and jewels and store of money. On hearing this, the anger of the husband was great; but he checked himself, and inquired which road the messenger from Kailása had taken, saying that he wished to follow him with a further message for his parents. So she very readily pointed out the direction in which the rogue had gone. With rage in his heart at the trick played upon his stupid wife, he rode off in hot haste, and after having proceeded a considerable distance, he caught sight of the flying rogue, who, finding escape hopeless, climbed up into a *pipal* tree.

The husband soon reached the foot of the
tree, when he shouted to the rogue to come
down. " No, I cannot," said he ; "this is the
way to Kailása," and then climbed to the very
top of the tree.   Seeing there was no chance
of the rogue coming down, and there being
no one near to whom he could call for help,
the old miser tied his horse to a neighbouring
tree, and began to climb up the *pipal* himself.
When the rogue observed this, he thanked all
his gods most fervently, and having waited
until his enemy had climbed nearly up to him,
he threw down his bundle of booty, and then
leapt nimbly from branch to branch till he
reached the ground in safety, when he mounted
the miser's horse and with his bundle rode
into a thick forest, where he was not likely
to be discovered.   Being thus balked the
miser came down the *pipal* tree slowly, cursing his own stupidity in having risked his
horse to recover the things which his wife had
given the rogue, and returned home at leisure.
His wife, who was waiting his return,
welcomed him with a joyous countenance, and
cried, "I thought as much: you have sent
away your horse to Kailása, to be used by
your old father."   Vexed at his wife's words,
as he was, he replied in the affirmative, to
conceal his own folly.

Through the Tamils it is probable this story reached Ceylon, where it exists in a slightly different form : A young girl, named Kaluhámi, had lately died, when a beggar came to the parents' house, and on being asked by the mother where he had come from, he said that he had just come from the other world to this world, meaning that he had only just recovered from severe illness. " Then," said the woman, " since you have come from the other world, you must have seen my daughter Kaluhámi there, who died but a few days ago. Pray tell me how she is." The beggar, seeing how simple she was, replied, " She is my wife, and lives with me at present, and she has sent me to you for her dowry." The woman at once gave him all the money and jewels that were in the house, and sent him away delighted with his unexpected good luck. Soon after, the woman's husband returned, and learning how silly she had been, mounted his horse and rode after the beggar. The rest of the story corresponds to the Tamil version, as above, with the exception that when the husband saw the beggar slide down the tree, get on his horse, and ride off, he cried out to him, " Hey, son-in-law, you may tell Kaluhámi that the money and jewels are from her mother, and that the horse is from me;" which is altogether inconsistent, since he is represented as the reverse of a simpleton in pursuing the beggar, on hearing what his wife had done. It is curious, also, to observe that in the Tamil version the man goes to the house with the deliberate purpose of deceiving the simple woman, while in the Sinhalese the beggar is evidently tempted by her mistaking the meaning of his words. But both present very close points of resemblance to the Norwegian story of the pretended pilgrim from paradise. There are indeed few instances of a story having travelled so far and lost so little of its original details, allowing for the inevitable local colouring.

APPENDIX.

HE idea ot the old English jest-book, *Jacke of Dover His Quest of Inquirie, or His Privy Search for the Veriest Foole in England* (London: 1604), may perhaps have been suggested by such popular tales as those of the man going about in quest of three greater fools than his wife, father-in-law, and mother-in-law. It is, however, simply a collection ot humorous anecdotes, not specially examples of folly or stupidity, most of which are found in earlier jest-books. The introduction is rather curious:

"When merry Jacke of Dover had made his privy search for the Foole of all Fooles, and making his inquirie in most of the principal places in England, at his return home he was adjudged to be the fool himself; but now wearied with the motley coxcombe, he hath undertaken in some place or other to find a verier foole than himself. But

first of all, coming to London, he went into
Paul's Church, where walking very melan-
choly in the middle aisle with Captain
Thingut and his fellowes, he was invited to
dine at Duke Humphry's ordinary,[1] where,
amongst other good stomachs that repaired
to his bountiful feast, there came a whole
jury of penniless poets, who being fellows of
a merry disposition (but as necessary in a
commonwealth as a candle in a straw bed),
he accepted of their company, and as from
poets cometh all kind of folly, so he hoped
by their good directions to find out his Foole
of Fooles, so long looked for. So, thinking
to pass away the dinner-hour with some
pleasant chat (lest, being overcloyed with too
many dishes, they should surfeit), he discovered to them his merry meaning, who,
being glad of so good an occasion of mirth,
instead of a cup of sack and sugar for diges-
tion, these men of little wit began to make
inquiry and to search for the aforesaid fool,
thinking it a deed of charity to ease him of so
great a burden as his motley coxcomb was,
and because such weak brains as are now
resident almost in every place, might take

[1] In the nave of St. Paul's (says Timbs, in his
Curiosities of Old London) was the tomb of Sir
John Beauchamp, son of Guy, Earl of Warwick:
it was unaccountably called "Duke Humphrey's
Tomb," and the dinnerless persons who lounged
here were said to dine with Duke Humphrey.

benefit hereat. In this manner began the inquiry :

The Foole of Hereford.

" ' Upon a time (quoth one of the jury) it was my chance to be in the city of Hereford, when, lodging at an inn, I was told of a certain silly-witted gentleman there dwelling, that would assuredly believe all things that he heard for a truth ; to whose house I went upon a sleeveless errand, and finding occasion to be acquainted with him, I was well entertained, and for three days' space had my bed and board in his house ; where, amongst many other fooleries, I, being a traveller, made him believe that the steeple of Brentwood, in Essex, sailed in one night as far as Calais, in France, and afterwards returned again to its proper place. Another time I made him believe that in the forest of Sherwood, in Nottinghamshire, were seen five hundred of the King of Spain's galleys, which went to besiege Robin Hood's Well, and that forty thousand scholars with elder squirts performed such a piece of service as they were all in a manner taken and overthrown in the forest. Another time I made him believe that Westminster Hall, for suspicion of treason, was banished for ten years into Staffordshire. And last of all, I made him believe that a tinker should be baited to death at Canterbury for getting two and twenty children in a year; whereupon, to prove me a liar, he took his horse and rode thither, and I, to verify him a fool, took my horse and rode hither.'

"'Well,' quoth Jacke of Dover, 'this in my mind was pretty foolery, but yet the Foole of all Fooles is not here found that I looked for.'

The Fool of Huntington.

"'And it was my chance (quoth another of the jury) upon a time to be at Huntington, where I heard tell of a simple shoemaker there dwelling, who having two little boys whom he made a vaunt to bring up to learning, the better to maintain themselves when they were men; and having kept them a year or two at school, he examined them saying, "My good boy," quoth he to one of them, "what dost thou learn and where is thy lesson?" "O father," said the boy, "I am past grace." "And where art thou?" quoth he to the other boy, who likewise answered that he was at the devil and all his works. "Now Lord bless us," quoth the shoemaker, "whither are my children learning? The one is already past grace and the other at the devil(and all his works !" Whereupon he took them both from school and set them to his own occupation.¹'"

A number of others of the jury of penniless poets having related their stories, at last it is agreed that if the Foole of all Fooles cannot be found among those before named, one of themselves must be the fool, for there cannot be a verier fool than a poet, " for poets have good wits, but cannot use them, great store of money, but cannot keep it," etc.

It is doubtful what the name " Jack of Dover" imports, as that of the imaginary inquirer after fools. The author of the Cook's Tale of Gamelyn—which is generally considered as a spurious " Canterbury ' tale— represents, in the prologue, mine [host of the Tabard as saying to Roger the Cook :

¹ The jest is thus told in some parts of Scotland : An old gentleman, walking in the country, met three small boys on their way home from school, and asked them how they progressed in their learning. The youngest—referring, of course, to the *Shorter Catechism*—replied that he was "in a state of sin and misery;" the second, that he was past " redemption ; " and the eldest, that he was "in the pains of hell for ever."

" Full many a pastie hast thou lettin blode ;
    And many a jack of Dovyr hast thou sold,
    That hath ben twicè hot and twicè cold."

Dr. Brewer says—apparently on the strength
of these lines — that a " Jack of Dover "
is a fish that has been cooked a second time.
But it may have been a name of a particular
kind of fish caught in the waters off Dover.
If, however, a " Jack of Dover " is a twice-
cooked fish, the title of the jest-book is not
inappropriate, since all the stories it com-
prises are at least " twice-told."

INDEX.

Abdera, Man of, 6.
Alewife and her Hens, 73.
Alfonsus, Peter, 45.
Arab and his Cow, 70.
Arab Schoolmaster, 83.
Arabian Idiot, 133.
Arabian Nights, 81, 83, 133, 146.
Arabian Noodles, 70, 75, 107, 147.
Armstrong's, Archie, *Banquet of Jests*, 74.
Ashton, John, xiv.
Ass and the Two Sharpers, 81.
Austwick, Carles of, 17, 53, 54.
Avadánas, 53.

Babrius, 53.
Bakki, Brothers of, 32, 64.
Bang-eater and his Wife, 147.
Bang-eaters and the Dogs, 109.
Barrett, F. T., 9.
Barrin' o' the Door, 107.
Belmont, Fools of, 55.
Beryn, Tale of, 40.
Beschi, Father, 29.
Bharataka Dwatrinsati, 158.
Bigarrures of the Sieur Gaulard, 8, 12, 20, 76.
Bidpai's Fables, 53.
Birth-Stories—*see* Játakas.
Boccaccio's *Decameron*, 39.

"Boiling" River, 30, 43.
Bond, The Lord's, 17.
Borde, Andrew, 23.
Bráhmans, Four Simple, 171.
Bromyard, John, 167.
Buddha's Five Precepts, 69.
Bull and the Gate, 54.
Bull of Siva, 48.
Burton's *Arabian Nights*, 83.
Busk's *Folk-Lore of Rome*, 204.
Butter eaten by a Dog, 18.
Buzzard, The Gothamite's, 38.

Cabbage-Tree, 47.
Caftan on Tree, 90.
Calf's Head in a Pot, 89.
Campbell's *Popular Tales of the West Highlands*, 32, 33, 34, 35, 36, 154, 193.
Cat and old Woman, 65.
Cat, Men of Schilda's, 61.
Cazotte's *New Arabian Nights*, 133.
Ceylon — *see* Sinhalese Noodles.
Chamberlain, B. H., 130.
Cheese, The Gothamite's, 34.
Cheese on the Highway, 40.
Cheese, The Stolen, 91.
Chinese Noodles, 93, 94.
Coelho's *Contes Portuguezes*, 120.

15

Colombo, Michele, 81.
Conde Lucanor, 162.
Countryman and Dog, 79.
Cozens, F. W., 9.
Council-House, Dark, 57.
Crane's *Italian Popular Tales,* 117, 128, 139, 202, 204.
Cuckoo, Hedging in the, 26.
Cumeans and the bath, 4; and the father's corpse, 15; and the fig-tree, 10; and the pot of honey, 19; and the stolen clothes, 4.
Dark Council-House, 57.
Dasent's *Norse Tales,* 126, 212.
Dekker's *Gul's Horn Book,* 26.
Devil in the Meadow, 42.
Disciplina Clericalis, 45.
Doctor and Patients, 5.
Doctor's Apprentice, 168.
Dog that ate Honey, 18.
Door, Taking Care of the, 97, 98.
Dreams, The Good, 92, 93.
Dubois, Abbé, 171.
Duke Humphrey, Dining with, 220.

Ear, Biting one's own, 86.
Eberhard's *Hieraclis,* 3.
Eel, Drowning the, 33.
English typical booby, 139.

Fabliaux, Le Grand s, 39, 163.
Family, Best of the, 165.
Farmer and his Pigs, 54.
Fisher, Indian Silly Son as, 163.
Fishers, Gothamite, 28.
Fleas, Bit by, 14.
Folk-Lore in Southern India, 212.
Fool and the aloes-wood, 98; and the birch-tree, 151; and the cotton, 99; and the cup lost in the sea, 99; and the elephant-driver, 51; and his porridge, 119; and the *Ramayana,* 70;

and the sack of meal, 19, 25, 68; and the shop-keeper, 100; at his fire-side, 119; kicked by his mule, 119; of Hereford, 221; of Huntingdon, 222.
Fools and the buffalo, 101; and the Bull of Siva, 48; and their inheritance, 118; and the mosquitoes, 95; and the palm-trees, 96; and the trunks, 96.
Fortini's Italian Novels, 162.
Fuller, Thomas, on the Gothamites, 20.
Furnivall, F. J., 23.

Gaulard, The Sieur, 8, 12, 20, 76.
Geese and Tortoise, 52.
Gesta Romanorum, 117, 163.
Gibb's *Forty Vazirs,* 109, 166, 167.
Giufà, the Sicilian Booby, 97, 139, 165.
Goat and Old Woman, 66.
Gooroo Paramartan, 29, 37, 157.
Gossips and their late Husbands, 74.
Gossips at the Alehouse, 40.
Gotham, Tales of the Mad Men of, xiii., 20, 24-44.
Grazzini's Florentine Fool, 161.
Grecian Noodles, 1-15.

Halliwell-Phillipps, J. O., xiii., 13, 22, 27, 53.
Hama and Hums, Men of, 75.
Hazlitt, W. C., xiii., 12.
Heaven, Sorry he has gone to, 74.
Herdsman, The Foolish, 106.
Herodotus, Stephens' *Apology* for, 119.
Hierokles, Jests of, 2
Hilopadesa, 162.
Honey, Pot of, 6, 18.
Hunter's Dream of a Boar, 4.

Icelandic Noodles, 32,64,163.
Indian Noodles, 29, 37, 44, 48, 51, 70, 96, 97-106, 111, 118, 158, 161, 163, 170, 212.
Italian Noodles, 115, 127, 143, 160, 197, 202, 204.
Irish Labourer and Farmer, 8.
Irishman and his ass, 119.
Irishman and his hens, 120.
Irishman and lost shovel, 99.
Irishmen and mosquitoes, 14.
Irishman's Dream, 92.

Jack of Dover's Quest, 219.
Japanese Noodle, 130.
Jâtakas (Buddhist Birth-Stories), 52, 65, 95, 164.
Jests of Scogin, 162.
Joe Miller's Jest-Book, 1, 2.
Judge and Thieves, 87.

Kabail Tales, 37, 154.
Kashmiri Tales, 65, 89, 111.
Kathá Manjari, 11, 70, 100, 163.
Kathá Sarit Ságara, 48, 53, 120, 164.
Kerchief, The, 90.
Khoja Nasr-ed-Din, 89.
King's Stupid Son, The, 167.
Knife, The Gothamites', 53.
Knowles, J. H., 66, 113.

Laird of Logan, 13.
Leger's *Contes Populaires Slaves*, 128, 154.

Marie de France, 46.
Mery Tales and Quicke Answeres, 161.
Miller's Jest-Book, 1, 2.
Millstone of the Schildburgers, 59.
Minstrel and Pupil, 166.
Mork Transformed, 81.
Moon a green cheese, 44.
Moon in the well, 92.

Moon swallowed by an ass 46.
"Mortuus Loquens," 160.
Mummy, The, 15.

Nasr-ed-Din Khoja, 89.
Natesa Sastri Pandit, 212.
Needham's *Hierocles*, 3.
Noodles, The Three Great, 191.
Norfolk Noodles, 17.
Norse Noodles, 123, 207.
Notts Bridge, 24.

Orientalist, The, 69, 87, 114, 143, 160.

Pancha Tantra, 67, 171.
Paradise, Man who came from, 204, 210, 212, 217.
Pedant, bald man, and barber, 6; and the lost book, 13; and his dream, 5, 6; and the jar of feathers, 5; and his jar of wine, 9; and the mirror, 9; and the two slave-boys, 4; and his slave who died, 8; and the sparrows, 5; and the twin-brothers, 12; and his tomb, 8.
Persian Noodle, 7.
Persian Tales, 7, 66, 79.
Philotimus, 27.
Poet and the Dogs, 79.
Poggius' *Facetiæ*, 160, 162.
Priest of Gotham, 42.
Princess caused to grow, 102
Pupil, The Attentive, 165.

Ralston's *Russian Folk Tales*, 48, 153.
Relic-hunter, 95.
Rents of Gothamites, 27.
Right Hand or Left, 91.
River, "Boiling," 30, 43.
Rivière's *Contes Populaires de la Kabylie du Djurdjura*, 37, 154.

Russian Noodles, 47, 128, 151, 154, 195.
Rustic and the Dog, 79.

Sacke Full of Newes, 46, 97.
Sa'dí's *Gulistán*, xi, 79.
Schilda, The Men of, 56.
Schoolmaster's Lady-love, 83.
Sesame, Roasted, 120.
Sheep's Eyes, Casting, 41, 126, 127.
Sicilian Boobies, 97, 116, 139, 165.
Silent Noodles, 107—117.
Silly Matt, 123.
Silly Son, The, 121.
Simple Simon, 121, 122.
Simpleton and Sharpers, 81.
Sindibád Náma, 66.
Sinhalese Noodles, 67-69, 87, 89, 113, 141, 165, 179, 217.
Smith, Alexander, 9.
Spade, The Stolen, 94.
Spinning-Wheel, The, 36.
Stephens, Henry, Tales by, 119.
Stokes' *Indian Fairy Tales*, 154.
Summa Prædicantium, The, 167.

Tabourot, Etienne, 8.
Tales and Quicke Answeres, 161.

Tawney, C. H., 48.
Taylor's *Wit and Mirth*, 9, 10, 74, 78.
Thief on a Tree, 11.
Thoms, W. J., xii., 56.
Thoroton's *History of Nottinghamshire*, 21.
Three Greatest Noodles, 191.
Treasure Trove, 144, 151, 154.
Trivet, The Gothamite's, 36.
Turkish Noodles, 11, 86, 90, 93, 109, 166, 167.
Twelve Fishers, The, 28.
Twin Brothers, 12.

Vives, Ludovicus, 46.

Warton's *History of English Poetry*, 22.
Washerman and his young Ass, 103.
Wasp's Nest, 40.
"Whittle to the Tree," 53.
Widows, The Two, 74.
Wiltshire Noodles, 17, 54.
Wither's *Abuses Whipt and Stript*, 26.
Wolf's Tail, The, 91.
Wood, Anthony, on the Gotham Tales, 23.
Worsted Balls, The, 35.
Wrestler and the Wag, 7.
Wrong Man wakened, 6, 7.

www.ingramcontent.com/pod-product-compliance
Lightning Source LLC
Chambersburg PA
CBHW030815020726
47499CB00006B/1919